Jamming the Classroom

Jamming the Classroom

Musical Improvisation and Pedagogical Practice

Ajay Heble and Jesse Stewart

University of Michigan Press
Ann Arbor

Published in the United States of America by the
University of Michigan Press
Manufactured in the United States of America
Printed on acid-free paper
First published October 2023

A CIP catalog record for this book is available from the British Library.

Library of Congress Cataloging-in-Publication data has been applied for.

ISBN 978-0-472-07636-9 (hardcover : alk. paper)
ISBN 978-0-472-05636-1 (paper : alk. paper)
ISBN 978-0-472-90375-7 (open access ebook)

https://doi.org/10.3998/mpub.12733416

The University of Michigan Press's open access publishing program is made possible thanks to additional funding from the University of Michigan Office of the Provost and the generous support of contributing libraries.

In memory of Pauline Oliveros.

About the Cover Art

The image on the front cover of this book is by the artists at Being Studio (formerly H'Art of Ottawa), an organization in Ottawa, Canada, that facilitates art making among adults with developmental disabilities. In 2013–2014, Jesse Stewart collaborated with the artists at H'Art of Ottawa on a multimedia community-arts project titled *Turning the Page* (discussed in chapter 5 of this book). Inspired by the collaboration, the participants created paintings of various musical instruments on five-inch-square canvases that were assembled into the composite image shown on the front cover.

We love this image because it imagines an inclusive space in which a myriad of creative energies are brought into dialogue with one another: in addition to traditional instruments like trumpet, piano, and cello, it depicts experimental instruments such as the waterphone and Reactable, as well as musical found objects, including a cardboard box. The creativity, dialogue, and inclusivity embodied in this image are qualities that we want to encourage and cultivate in our teaching and through this book.

For more information on Being Studio, see www.beingstudio.ca.

Contents

Preface

"Stepping into Another World"

"When you play music in this world, you're actually stepping into another world," explains improvising bassist William Parker in a February 2021 *New York Times* article about his lifework and his music.[1] "No matter what's happening with you, whether you owe 10 months' rent, or you're dealing with some kind of mental anxiety or hardship, the music takes over."[2] The idea of stepping into another world seems an apt way to begin a book that seeks to make the case that teaching and learning musical improvisation can offer vital opportunities for imagining, creating, and enacting alternative ways of knowing, being, and living in the world. Drawing our inspiration from the work of improvising artists who, time and time again, have taught us how to turn dark curves into brilliant corners, how to take discouraging places and turn them into resonant spaces, we look to the pedagogy of improvisation as an opportunity to step into another world.

Little did we imagine when we were writing this book that we'd be readying our manuscript for submission to the press during a pandemic that necessitated a worldwide collective improvisation. Little did we imagine that the debates with which we've been engaging throughout our research and writing, and the questions we've sought to raise about the critical and pedagogical practices of musical improvisation, would be turned on their head when, in response to Covid-19, we'd be asked to shelter in place, forced to practice social distancing, forced to cancel gigs and workshops, and required to teach remotely over a computer screen rather than in the face-to-settings to which we were accustomed. Little did we imagine that the kinds of public events that are often so vital a part of community-engaged improvisatory work wouldn't be possible for well over a year. Little could we have imagined this new world into which we'd be stepping.

As we think about these challenges, we're reminded of Rebecca Solnit's work documenting the profound sense of resilience that has emerged out of the extraordinary communities and improvised responses found amid situations of devastation, such as those in post-Katrina New Orleans. In her 2009 book *A Paradise Built in Hell: The Extraordinary Communities That Arise in Disaster*, Solnit quotes from Kathleen Tierney, director of the University of Colorado's Natural Hazards Center from 2003 to 2016:

> [Decades of studying disaster have] made me far more interested in people's own capacity for self-organizing and for improvising. You come to realize that people often do best when they're not following a script or a score but when they're improvising and coming up with new riffs, and I see this tremendous creativity in disaster responses both on the part of community residents and on the part of good emergency personnel—seeing them become more flexible, seeing them break rules, seeing them use their ingenuity in the moment to help restore the community and to protect life, human life, and care for victims. It is when people deviate from the script that exciting things happen.[3]

Exciting things happen when people deviate from musical scripts too. Indeed, musical improvisation has long been an important catalyst for imagining—and enacting—new ways of living together in the world when we deviate from a predetermined script or score.

Social theorist Jacques Attali famously wrote in his book *Noise* about music's annunciatory force, its ability to foreshadow "new relations among people."[4] Amid the unprecedented global challenges caused by the Covid-19 pandemic, the legacy of colonization, the climate emergency, and profound systemic inequality, music has offered us some inspirational moments of resourcefulness, resilience, and hope. Working without a written score or script, improvising musicians have shown us throughout the pandemic, as they have shown us before, how they can use the resources at hand to make right things transpire, sometimes in even the most challenging circumstances (see Fischlin, Heble, and Lipsitz). Indeed, the current moment has made the arguments we make in this book—about improvisation's capacity to cultivate hope and envision a more just society—seem even more necessary, more urgent.

Some of our own experiences during the pandemic have reminded us of improvisation's capacity to inspire and to restore a sense of community in uncertain times. At the outset of the pandemic, I (Jesse) posted a series of forty daily videos on Facebook that featured short improvised musical performances on different instruments, including a variety of found objects (stones, seashells, a saw blade, a kitchen sink, and so forth). Some of these videos, particularly the found object improvisations, were shared and viewed thousands of times. Dozens of educators around the world indicated that they were inspired by the videos to incorporate found object improvisation into the music lessons that they were delivering online. What started as something ostensibly for my friends turned into something much larger, with one of the videos (an improvisation on wooden canoe paddles) being viewed over thirty thousand times. The reach of this work was completely unexpected, as was its capacity to make connections and to assist other educators during a challenging period of social isolation. Judging from the hundreds of comments I received, as well as the dozens of audio and video recordings that educators and parents shared with me of young people developing their own found object improvisations, it seems as though the videos were of pedagogical value in addition to being a way for people stuck at home to pass the time.

In summer 2020, I (Ajay) organized a twenty-four-hour online festival of improvised arts known as "IF" (Improvisation Festival) that featured over 150 artists and attracted a global audience of more than five thousand viewers. Second and third editions of IF were created for online delivery in August 2021 and August 2022, making for three substantial festival experiences centering on improvising voices from across the globe. While in-person arts festivals were being canceled, the IF events offered a compelling alternative for people from around the world to come together and find solace and inspiration through art. The festival taught important lessons about creativity and resilience; about how improvisational artists can thrive using whatever materials they have at their disposal, adapting artistically to the environments and circumstances in which they find themselves; and about the role improvisational artistic practices can play in modeling alternative ways of being together and collaborating in community, even while we remain apart. If festivals, as we suggest later in this book, might be thought of as complex, publicly facing pedagogical acts or, in arts consultant Max Wyman's terms, as "testing grounds for new visions of how we live together, new ways to establish shared values,"[5] then the experience of staging IF demonstrated the power of improvisational responses, of creatively using public spaces and the digital sphere to connect artists with their communities—and to develop new ones—across time and space. A core component of the digital sphere that made it possible for participants during IF to forge a vibrant and powerful sense of community and to transcend the limits associated with in-person festivals, was the chat feature of many online platforms. As philosopher Eric Lewis and arts presenter Christos Carras (both of whom were involved in the IF Festival) note in their coauthored essay on performance-based arts during Covid, the ability of audiences (and, we would add, artists) to ask questions or to engage in discussion via the chat room can play "a crucial role in pandemic performance, helping build connections between artists and audiences, and create spatially dispersed communities of the type that live performances cannot. A spatially distanced and isolated fan of a particular performer," they suggest, "can now 'attend' a performance wherever they may be and interact with the performer and other fans. One often gets to see performers in their living rooms and gain a sense of intimacy and familiarity different from that of staged live performances. If you follow the chatroom feeds during performances you often discover that they supply background information about the performances, advertise future performances, and introduce individual fans to each other—you can witness community-in-formation."[6]

Our own community-in-formation experiences during the pandemic have made it clear to us how the current moment has prompted new and adapted pedagogies of musical improvisation, how it has provided new ways of thinking about, and expanding the reach of, the work we do when we improvise musically. To quote Lewis and Carras again, the pandemic, "for all the ways it has negatively impacted the cultural sector, has also opened up new opportunities for rethinking what it means to present performance-based arts; what the role of an audience could, or should, be; how artistic collaborations might take place; and more generally what constitutes and animates an increasingly global artistic community."[7]

Indeed, the idea that improvisation, as both a vital creative practice and a mode of being in the world, has significant pedagogical lessons to teach as we respond to the Covid-19 emergency and the myriad of other challenges we currently face is explored in two special volumes titled "Improvisation, Musical Communities, and COVID-19" in the journal *Critical Studies in Improvisation*. Guest editors Daniel Fischlin, Laura Risk, and Jesse Stewart suggest that "to play music, and particularly to improvise, is to engage with states of ongoing precarity: how, exactly, the next note will sound, or even what it may be, is unknown—until it is not, and the following note is what hangs on the knife edge. The resilience of improvisational musicians, of all kinds, in the face of the pandemic," they argue, "points to their disciplined acquaintance with creating on that edge." They continue: "While the wreckage [from the pandemic] is obvious, the resilience of the most fragile forms of the musical socius present[s] remarkable examples of survival. Many of the tactics deployed by venues, performers, and community organizers are deeply connected with the improvisatory forms of practice found in the music they host, perform, and/or use for wider projects of social engagement."[8]

As we think about the current moment in relation to the arguments we present in the pages that follow, we're inclined to ask some preliminary questions.

How have the tactics that emerged in response to the pandemic shaped our pedagogy? How might the move to online pedagogies of improvisation change the ways in which improvised musical practices are being taught, discussed, and written about, even in a postpandemic landscape? To what extent do we need radically to rethink our teaching and learning practices? Indeed, what does it mean to create on the edge, and how might we foster pedagogical practices that enable such creation? Additionally, how might improvisation play a role in the new face of "arts-based community making" both online and in a postpandemic society? People are learning to improvise with new technologies, and they are participating in new ways of knowing and learning increasingly in digital spaces, rather than face-to-face. What role does—or can—improvisation play in these contexts, and how might improvisational music pedagogies help facilitate some of these cultural and historic shifts?

The physical-distancing measures prompted by the pandemic have posed notable challenges for musicians, as most opportunities to perform or hear live music were eliminated virtually overnight. In response, many musicians have offered livestreamed musical performances on Facebook, YouTube, and other streaming platforms. Greater numbers of improvising musicians began exploring telematic or networked modes of improvisation through online platforms such as Zoom, Jamkazam, Jamulus, JackTrip, Syncspace, and others. Several arts organizations and academic institutions have made considerable advances in networked musical performance and related research during the pandemic, including NowNet Arts in New York, the SoundWIRE Research Group within the Center for Computer Research in Music and Acoustics at Stanford University, the Sonic Arts Research Centre at Queen's University

Belfast, and the Online Musical Ensemble Research project at Carleton University in Ottawa, Canada. By modeling new ways of improvising online, these organizations are developing new forms of improvisation pedagogy that will have a lasting impact on the ways in which we teach and learn improvisation.

Yet the world changed in other significant ways during the pandemic. In May 2020, the brutal murder of George Floyd by Minneapolis police sparked outrage and mass protests around the world. In the months since, millions of protesters from diverse age, gender, and racial backgrounds have come together to protest police violence and systemic racism under the banner of the Black Lives Matter movement. In Canada, the discovery, beginning in 2021, of mass graves of murdered Indigenous children at the sites of former residential schools has prompted widespread protests and a national reckoning of Canada's colonial and genocidal past. What does it mean to improvise (and to teach improvisation) during a time when many of us are seeking to find appropriate ways to express our solidarity with Black and Indigenous communities, and with the protesters who have been standing up against systemic and structural racism?

It seems clear that the question posed by Martin Luther King Jr. in the title of his 1967 book, *Where Do We Go from Here: Chaos or Community?*, is as relevant and as urgent today as it was when Dr. King first published it. Might improvisation, we wonder, help, even in some modest way, to turn spectators into actors, to bring about the radical revolution in values that Dr. King felt was necessary to guarantee the presence of justice? "No great victories are won in a war for the transformation of a whole people without total participation," he argued. "Less than this will not create a new society; it will only evoke more sophisticated token amelioration."[9] It's worth noting that many aspects of the protests have been improvisatory. From groups of protesters forming human walls to shield vulnerable individuals from harm to suburban dads using cordless leaf blowers to repel tear gas used by federal agents, protesters have made split-second decisions to enact an ethic of care for one another and, in some cases, for members of the opposition.[10]

What, then, might we learn from being, teaching, and improvising in the current moment? And what might this moment teach us in the larger context in which improvisation has been a sustained strategy in a tool kit that includes pedagogical experiences writ large? Many thinkers, writing in a range of contexts, have begun to take up a related set of questions. Paul Loeb, in a piece called "Coronavirus as a Teachable

Classroom Moment: Engaging Students across the Curriculum," says it's understandable that both teachers and students are feeling overwhelmed during these challenging times. "But," he says, "the COVID-19 crisis also gives a chance for students, and all of us, to have a sense of purpose. We can use classroom conversations to try and understand the choices that led to our current situation and the choices being made to address it. And then encourage students to voice their views on the critical continuing decisions."[11] And in another essay responding to the pandemic, "Teaching African American Literature during COVID-19," Farah Jasmine Griffin makes a related claim: "This moment," she says, "has allowed us to work together in a different way. The crisis stopped us in our tracks, but it also provided an opportunity."[12] Like Loeb, she, too, sees potential and possibility during these times. She references author and activist Arundhati Roy's now much-cited article, "The Pandemic Is a Portal": "Historically," says Roy,

> pandemics have forced humans to break with the past and imagine their world anew. This one is no different. It is a portal, a gateway between one world and the next. We can choose to walk through it, dragging the carcasses of our prejudice and hatred, our avarice, our data banks and dead ideas, our dead rivers and smoky skies behind us. Or we can walk through lightly, with little luggage, ready to imagine another world. And ready to fight for it.[13]

In a blog post entitled "The Single Most Essential Requirement in Designing a Fall Online Course," Cathy Davidson emphasizes that, in these challenging and unprecedented times of the pandemic, we (as teachers and students) "are learning from a place of dislocation, anxiety, uncertainty, awareness of social injustice, anger, and trauma."[14] The disruption of our lives in this historical moment, she suggests, needs to be the starting point for thinking about how and why we will teach online "because education is an excellent way of moving beyond trauma to a place of agency, confidence, control, community, care, activism, and contribution."[15]

Consider the claims that these thinkers have been putting forward: Working together in a different way (Griffin). Learning from a place of disruption and moving to a place of agency, confidence, control, community, care, activism, and contribution (Davidson). Imagining the world anew (Roy). A teachable moment (Loeb). A radical revolution in values and in the organization of society (King). And think again of William Parker's assertion about stepping into another world. How, we wonder, might we use these assertions as prompts to think through the ways in which the dual pandemics of Covid-19 and systemic racism have shown us that the ability to improvise, to respond to unforeseen circumstances, has never been more important?

One of our central arguments throughout this book is that musical improvisation has much to teach us about social and societal improvisation, about the ways in which we listen to—and interact with—one another across various forms of difference. Improvisation offers strategies for managing and responding to change. So where, to invoke again the title of Dr. King's 1967 book, do we go from here? And in what ways might pedagogies of improvisation figure in our efforts to imagine the world anew?

There is no doubt that we live in challenging times. But challenges can also, as so many artists in the history of improvised music have made so clear, lead to opportunities and lessons about how we might live our lives differently. In their book *Playing for Keeps: Improvisation in the Aftermath*, Daniel Fischlin and Eric Porter argue that "in the aftermath of chaos and trauma, improvisatory modes of being provide generative alternatives based on risk taking and nonconformity rooted in cocreative connections."[16] "Improvisation," they suggest, "is not the answer, then, but a tool to create flexible, site-specific strategies that connect the creative and the critical—that negotiate stricture and unrealized possibility."[17] The strictures of the current moment are manifold. But so too are the unrealized possibilities that improvisation offers. In challenging us to adapt to unprecedented circumstances, we have been offered a kind of call to action. Imagining the world anew is no easy task. It's not always comfortable to step into another world, to let go of what we know and expect, to abandon the tried and true, or to trade the pleasures of certitude and fixity for the surprises that come from ways of knowing (and ways of being) that can't readily be accommodated within received frameworks of assumption. How we respond to this call to action may be one of the most urgent predicaments and pedagogical imperatives confronting us today.

If there has ever been a moment in our history that demands improvisation, surely, we are living it.

Acknowledgments

This book has been a long time a-coming, and we'd like to acknowledge the tremendous support and guidance we've received from many people during the time we've been planning, writing, revising, and readying the book for publication.

Sincere thanks to the team at University of Michigan Press, especially to our editor Sara Cohen for her enthusiastic response to our inquiries and for expertly guiding us through the process. To the series editors for Music and Social Justice, Will Cheng and Andrew Dell'Antonio: we are so grateful to be working with you. We've benefited from the inspired comments and highly resonant suggestions you've offered us. Thanks, too, to all our anonymous peer reviewers for the careful reading and perspicacious feedback.

We're also hugely grateful to have had the opportunity to work with, and to get to know, many of the amazing improvising musicians whose artistry is discussed in this book. We would, in particular, like to extend our thanks to the artists who took the time to speak with us about their work: Norman Adams, Anne Bourne, Jane Bunnett, Jean Derome, Hamid Drake, Douglas Ewart, Jaron Freeman-Fox, François Houle, Susie Ibarra, Dong-Won Kim, George Lewis, David Mott, Éric Normand, Pauline Oliveros (1932–2016), Evan Parker, William Parker, Eddie Prévost, and Marianne Trudel.

Much of our work, including this book, has been made possible as a result of generous support from the Social Sciences and Humanities Research Council of Canada (SSHRC) through its Partnership Grant program. Headquartered at the International Institute for Critical Studies in Improvisation (IICSI), a partnered research institute supported by SSHRC, much of our research on improvisation has drawn on, and been improved by, the care and support offered by IICSI staff and by generous and ongoing intellectual exchanges with our many friends and colleagues who have been affiliated with the institute. Big shout-outs to Sam Boer, Daniel Fischlin, Liz Jackson, Mark Laver, Eric Lewis, George Lewis, George Lipsitz, Sheetal Lodhia, Justine Richardson, Shawn Van Sluys, Ellen Waterman, and Marie Zimmerman. We've also benefited from the support we received for this book from our three wonderful graduate research assistants, Erin Felepchuk, Jeannette Hicks, and Chris Worden.

A very special shout-out to former IICSI staff member Rachel Collins. Rachel offered unwavering support to us during many aspects of this book's preparation. Her eye for detail, her organizational skills, and her keen problem-solving abilities have contributed to a wonderful and astonishingly productive working environment. Her energy and commitments have inspired and challenged us to do our best work.

Ajay offers sincere thanks to Dr. Eric Schnell for his extraordinary improvisation, and to Malcolm Campbell and Karina McInnis for their continuing support.

And, as always, we acknowledge that none of our work would be possible without the love, guidance, care, support, and friendship we receive from our families. Special thanks to Sheila and Michele.

Introduction

The Many Classrooms of Improvisation

> There are many classrooms: the ones in the university, the one in
> grandma's kitchen, and the bigger one called life. School doesn't teach
> us the secrets of creativity. School prepares us to not be afraid of the
> secrets when we run across them, to interpret the scrolls left by the
> ancients and to recognize the songs of birds and other sound makers
> who live in nature, drawing inspiration from them.
>
> —William Parker

The epigraph above comes from bassist William Parker's liner notes to *Anagrams*, a 2014 recording of improvised music by baritone saxophonist David Mott and percussionist Jesse Stewart. With characteristic poeticism and insight, Parker reminds us that learning takes place in many locations, both formal (e.g., the university) and informal (e.g., grandma's kitchen), and in diverse ways that include learning from the past, learning from the environment, and learning from our life experiences generally. We learn in and through each of these (and many other) classrooms and, crucially, through our navigations between and among them. For the most part, we wend our way through life's many classrooms in an unpremeditated manner, listening more intently to some lessons than others. In other words, learning is a fundamentally improvisatory process. This is particularly true of the processes through which we learn to improvise musically.

What can we learn when we study musical improvisation? An approach to making music, certainly. One that emphasizes agency, creativity, dialogue, discovery, exploration, listening, risk, and responsibility. But we can learn more than that. We learn how to collaborate with others, to negotiate differences of various kinds through real-time, face-to-face (and, increasingly, through remote forms of) interaction within overlapping networks of musical, social, and pedagogical practice. This book examines these networks, parsing some of the varied pedagogical locations and methods through which we learn to improvise.

Following critical pedagogy theorist Henry Giroux, we understand pedagogy as "the complicated processes by which knowledge is produced, skills are learned meaningfully, identities are shaped, desires are mobilized, and critical dialogue becomes a central form of public interaction."[1] With this definition of pedagogy in mind, we want to examine the ways in which the teaching and learning of improvisational musical practices can be understood as vital and publicly resonant pedagogical acts that generate new forms of knowledge, new understandings of identity and community, and new imaginative possibilities. How, we want to ask, might the kinds of cultural and pedagogical institutions that present and promote improvised music shape our understanding of public culture, of memory, of history?[2]

In exploring these contexts and opening up these questions, our book is directed to a broad audience of both experienced and novice musical improvisers, scholars and students working across a wide spectrum of disciplines, and those interested in thinking about how improvised music can play an important role in experiential education and in what George Lipsitz refers to as "arts-based community-making." We draw on a mix of collaborative autoethnography, secondary literature, interviews with leading improvisers, and personal anecdotal material, and we bring a practical focus and orientation to ground our arguments. In much of what we present here, there's also an activist pedagogical orientation, a sense that musical improvisation has the powerful potential to function as a transformative social force. And as we seek to survey, through acts and practices of improvised music-making, some of the tools and concepts that can be used to build affirmative relations with others in community, we see our work here as being of particular interest to community activists and scholars of critical pedagogy.

In the pages that follow, we often draw on our own personal experiences not only as scholars and teachers, but also as musicians, arts presenters, festival organizers, and members of vibrant artistic and cultural communities. We hope, as William Cheng does in his book *Just Vibrations*, that "readers will feel free to scrutinize the book more, not less. Some writers, to be sure," notes Cheng, "still believe that academic and first-person narratives don't mix well. Feminist and queer theorists repeatedly run into accusations of narcissism, of overmixing the personal and the political. Disability scholars who admit their own hardships are likewise charged with indulging in 'moi-criticism,' appealing to emotions (and scoring so-called sympathy points) rather than to the intellect."[3] For us, the mix of academic and first-person narratives offers a compelling way to open discussion about musical improvisation and pedagogical practices. We remain mindful that, as Carolyn Ellis, Tony Adams, and Arthur Bochner suggest in their overview article on auto-ethnography, "the questions most important to autoethnographers are: who reads our work, how are they affected by it, and how does it keep a conversation going?"[4] So we'd like to take our cue from Ellis, Adams, and Bochner when they argue that "the autoethnographer not only tries to make personal experience meaningful and cultural experience engaging, but also, by producing accessible texts, she or he may be able to reach wider and more diverse . . . audiences that traditional research usually disregards, a move that can make personal and social change possible for more people."[5]

Interpreting the Scrolls

Over the past century, jazz has become an important locus for pedagogies of musical improvisation both inside the academy and out. Effectively denied access to many of the official institutions associated with music education, the progenitors of early jazz, swing, and bebop developed a variety of alternative pedagogical methods. These include various modes of self-teaching/learning, jam sessions, and apprenticeships in ensembles, all of which provided critically engaged means of developing a high level of musicianship and learning improvisatory skills. In the 1960s, there was a flourishing of community-based arts organizations committed to extending alternative pedagogies of jazz and improvised music, imbuing them with the imperatives of musical, economic, and social advancement within localized communities.[6] Since the 1970s, improvisatory practices associated with certain forms of jazz (notably "bebop" and its derivatives) have come to be widely taught at colleges and universities in North America and around the world.

Today, aspiring jazz musicians are able to access a wide variety of both self-directed and institution-based pedagogical resources. Such resources are amply documented and critically examined in the academic literature on jazz. See, for instance, Paul Berliner's *Thinking in Jazz*, David Ake's "Learning Jazz, Teaching Jazz," Tony Whyton's "Birth of the School: Discursive Methodologies in Jazz Education," and Ken Prouty's "The 'Finite' Art of Improvisation: Pedagogy and Power in Jazz Improvisation" and *Knowing Jazz: Community, Pedagogy, and Canon in the Information Age.* In addition, a wide variety of instructional materials on bebop-oriented jazz improvisation are now available, including the Jamey Aebersold (and other) series of play-along recordings and books such as Mark Levine's *The Jazz Theory Book* and Jim Grantham's *Jazzmaster Cookbook,* not to mention the bevvy of jazz instructional materials that are available online. We note also the widespread offering of jazz camps in recent years, including those designed specifically for girls, such as the annual Girls' Jazz and Blues Camp offered by the California Jazz Conservatory as well as the Jazz Camp for Girls in Denmark, which explicitly asks, "Can jazz improvisation as a teaching method help reduce the unequal gender balance in music?"[7]

In comparison, the pedagogical methods surrounding modes of improvisation that may be in dialogue with jazz and other genre-specific musical traditions, but nonetheless lie beyond them, have received relatively scant attention. Notable exceptions include David Borgo's "Free Jazz in the Classroom: An Ecological Approach to Music Education"; George Lewis's groundbreaking essay "Teaching Improvised Music: An Ethnographic Memoir"; Una MacGlone and Raymond MacDonald's "Learning to Improvise, Improvising to Learn"; Johansen, Holdhus, Larsson, and MacGlone's *Expanding the Space for Improvisation Pedagogy in Music: A Transdisciplinary Approach*; and the pedagogy-themed 2007 special issue of the journal *Critical Studies in Improvisation / Études critiques en improvisation.*[8] The edited collection by Ajay Heble and Mark Laver, *Musical Improvisation and Pedagogy: Beyond the Classroom,* which functions as something of a companion volume to this book, asks "how improvisation can breathe new life into old curricula; how it can help teachers and students to communicate more effectively; how it can break down damaging ideological boundaries between classrooms and communities; and how it can help students become more thoughtful, engaged, and activist global citizens."[9] All of these sources have animated the field of improvisation studies by encouraging a broadening, and a rethinking, of pedagogical and critical practices surrounding improvisation.

We've chosen our title, *Jamming the Classroom,* in an effort to reflect, and to build on the momentum of, this broader rethinking. We hope to make a critical intervention in the discourses and the practices surrounding music pedagogy in general, and pedagogies of improvised music in particular. The term "jamming" is generally used to describe what musicians do when they come together, often in informal or ad hoc performance or rehearsal situations, to play without a fully predetermined musical score. In his essay "Learning Jazz, Teaching Jazz," David Ake has written about the "importance of jam sessions as both a training ground and as a stage for demonstrating one's ability."[10] Discussing the broader pedagogical function that local jazz scenes have played in "setting norms for such aspects as jargon, codes of dress and public behaviour, and attitudes towards other musics and peoples,"[11] Ake suggests that "jam sessions play a central role in configuring and perpetuating this local education process," often audibly and visibly presenting "for beginning players what their particular jazz community expects of them, some or all of which might transfer to jazz scenes elsewhere."[12] Although Ake focuses on jam sessions within jazz communities specifically, many of his insights are relevant to jamming in other forms of musical improvisation as well.

In choosing our title for this book, we are mindful of Ake's insightful analysis of the pedagogical dimensions—both musical and otherwise—of jam sessions, as well as the work that other scholars have done in this area. But we're also very much drawn to the "perspective-jarring turnabout"[13] that author-activist and *Adbusters* cofounder Kalle Lasn intended to inspire by his use of the phrase "culture jamming" to describe various kinds of critical disruptions to mainstream epistemic orders. Drawing in part on the Situationists and their notion of the *détournement*, the subversion of elements in popular culture, Lasn's activist interventions into discourses promulgated by dominant knowledge-producing elites "sought to topple existing power structures and forge major adjustments to the way we live in the twenty-first century."[14]

What, then, does it mean to "jam the classroom," to speak of educational settings in terms of activist practices of critical and cultural intervention, and oppositional social movements? What does it mean to suggest, as William Parker does, that "there are many classrooms," and how do we activate these classrooms with the energies of critique and inspiration that have been such a vital part of the history of improvised music?[15] If we take our cue not just from the learning that goes on in conventional classrooms and credentialing institutions, but also from the work that happens in and through broader communities of practice, how do the improvisational practices of artists and the internal educational endeavors within community groups model—and enact— new forms of community-making and critical thinking? What does it mean to theorize the pedagogy of improvised music in relation to public programs of action, debate, and critical practice, and in the context of material practices and struggles for institutional authority?

In bringing together the teaching and learning of improvised music with oppositional social practices, we certainly don't mean to give the impression that all improvised music is necessarily activist in its orientation. Nor do we want to suggest that learning how to improvise musically will somehow automatically equate with critical disruptions to systems and structures of dominance and oppression. We've addressed these issues elsewhere in our work, and we've noted (and acknowledge again here) that we do need to put critical pressure on the utopian impulses of improvisation. We recognize that people who do bad things can (and do) also improvise, and that improvisation's effects won't always be celebratory, emancipatory, or socially just. However, as so many of the artists with whom we've collaborated over the years have made clear through their practice (and this is reflected in the interviews we conducted with them for this book), improvised music has clearly played an important role in cultivating a vital capacity for cocreation. The music, these artists are often quick to remind us, doesn't simply come out of nowhere; it has a history, and this history shapes how we listen to and understand the music, as well as how we engage with larger social and political concerns. In their book *Insubordinate Spaces: Improvisation and Accompaniment for Social Justice*, Barbara Tomlinson and George Lipsitz explain that while, in the popular understanding, improvisation "is often conceived of as an art based on the unleashing of private and personal impulses and desires, as an expression of the self that is indifferent to any social conventions or obligations," when practiced inside what they refer to as insubordinate spaces—places of possibility where members of subordinated social groups "can and do cultivate a collective capacity to discern the 'what can be' inside the 'what is'"[16]—improvisation, by contrast, "is a quintessentially social activity: a practice that requires working in concert with others through careful listening, responding, and collaborating."[17] This passage from Tomlinson and Lipsitz should make it clear that we aren't suggesting improvisation can be a utopian conduit to, or simple metaphor for, resilient and articulate selfhood. Nor we do want to imply that a societal emphasis on the habitual development/performance of a person's resilience/self-sufficiency (via improvisational creative practice) should impede larger agendas around equity by shifting responsibility for change from a collective to individual level, letting institutional and systemic abuses and imbalances off the hook. For us, it's important to understand musical improvisation as much more than simply an expression of individual impulses of selfhood; rather, our work—including this book—has been driven by a commitment to exploring improvisation as a vital social practice.[18] Quoting again from Tomlinson and Lipsitz: "Improvisation can make people alert, active, and empathetic. It assumes that ensembles can do more together than their members can do alone. It encourages participants to discern difficulties quickly and shift creatively. It challenges people to bring out the best in each other. Perhaps most important, it proceeds from the premise that human will and human work can transform the world."[19]

Transforming the world through will and through work is a grand call to action, we know. We know, too, that improvised music isn't likely to be the primary vehicle for bringing about such change. But at this time, when the degradations that continually threaten aggrieved populations have put the rights and the dreams of so many people around the globe at risk of being completely abandoned, we find ourselves inspired by such a call to action, moved by the very premise. And as we theorize improvisational musical practices in relation to publicly resonant pedagogical acts, we continue to be on the lookout for new forms of knowledge, new understandings of identity and community, new imaginative possibilities. Tomlinson and Lipsitz concur: "Insubordinate spaces," they write, "are places where acts of improvisation and accompaniment fuel the creation of new social relations and new social realities. At a time when corporations, governments, and philanthropic institutions have largely abandoned the masses, the peoples of the world have to find each other. They have to find value in undervalued things, places, and people. They must do so in many different ways in many different kinds of places: for instance, in women's centers and workers' centers, in college classrooms and community-based arts and education projects, in food co-ops, and in fights for fair housing."[20] Think again of William Parker's assertion about "many classrooms."

What, then, does it mean to jam the classroom? Increased institutional recognition, certainly. A recognition that seems particularly important, if belated, for a musical practice that continues to be largely disparaged and widely misunderstood both in the popular understanding and in more formal academic contexts of teaching and learning. But to jam the classroom means more than that. Paradoxically, even as it gains recognition within mainstream institutions (including classrooms in universities), improvisation needs to understood as a *critique* of dominant institutionalized assumptions and epistemic orders. We'll take up concerns related to the formal institutionalization of improvisation more fully later in the book. But for now, as we seek to tease out some of the implications of this paradox, we suggest a closer consideration of just why musical improvisation has been largely expunged from dominant models of pedagogical inquiry in both classrooms and communities.

In his essay "Beneath Improvisation," Vijay Iyer explains, "The decision to exclude improvisation as inherently unstable is not neutral, but is bound up with the endemic racism that has characterized social relations in the West and that is being brought to the fore in Black Lives Matter and other recent social and political movements."[21] He suggests that "the ongoing ejection of Black musics from the category of music aligns directly with the historic and ongoing dehumanization of Black people, the kind that was used to rationalize and justify enslavement, imperialism, plunder, and genocide on the timescale of the past half millennium."[22] Against the backdrop of institutionalized racism that Iyer describes, to jam the classroom is to argue for a renewed understanding of improvisation as both a musical and a social practice. To jam the classroom is to activate the knowledge and resources associated with improvisational practices in an expression of noncompliance with dominant orders of knowledge production. It is to recognize in the musical practices of aggrieved communities, and in particular of Black musicians, something far from the reaches of conventional forms of institutionalized power, yet something equally powerful, urgent, and expansive. It is to recognize that the teaching and learning of improvised music is about more than just a style or a set of musical skills; it can be part of an ongoing critique of dominant discourses, a critique that subjects the rigidity of white supremacy and racism (and other power asymmetries) to reformulation by articulating other ways of being, other ways of interacting within one another across difference, other possible futures. If we agree with historian Robin D. G. Kelley's assessment that "the most radical ideas often grow out of a concrete intellectual engagement with the problems of aggrieved populations confronting systems of oppression,"[23] then there is, we believe, much to be learned from the innovative models of improvisation developed by creative practitioners: lessons about the music's "social instrumentality,"[24] about how the social and creative antioppressive practices of aggrieved peoples can be enduring documents of hope, resilience, and determination.

In this book, we examine various forms of learning—individual, collaborative, institutional, and community-based—in order to understand current pedagogies of improvisation and to theorize possible new directions. We consider the pedagogy of musical improvisation not just in terms of the transmission of knowledges within classrooms and communities, but also as part of a broader activist practice that is grounded in knowledge that grows out of marginalized communities and that is articulated through forms of expression that derive much of their force, and their critical edge, from these communities.

Our book raises these considerations with particular focus on pedagogical practices surrounding modes of improvisatory musical discourse that are referred to variously as creative music/creative improvised music, free jazz, free improvisation, free music, open improvisation, nonidiomatic improvisation, and pan-idiomatic improvisation. There has been a significant amount of overlap and dialogue among these approaches to improvisation over the past sixty-plus years, as there is in the pages of this book. Furthermore, these terms, as the remarks we quoted from Vijay Iyer should remind us, are not neutral; rather, they have been used historically, and sometimes disparagingly, to frame improvised musical practices (and their associated pedagogies) in particular contexts and in particular ways. Moreover, these terms have done—and continue to do—important musical and pedagogical work both inside the classroom and out.

For example, the term "free" has been applied in various ways to improvisational musics emanating from diverse musical, social, and cultural settings over the past half century—from the "free jazz" of Ornette Coleman and Cecil Taylor, to the "free form" music of British saxophonist Joe Harriott, to the "free improvisation" of European improvisers including Derek Bailey, Evan Parker, Peter Brötzmann, Joëlle Léandre, Alexander von Schlippenbach, Maggie Nicols, Irène Schweizer, and others. However, the qualifier "free" has carried different meanings in each setting. For many European improvisers, free improvisation involves a process of real-time sonic exploration through the use of an ever-expanding range of so-called extended techniques and innovative modes of musical action and interaction. This approach to musical improvisation allows musicians to expand on (or depart from) conventional roles associated with particular instruments, and to reject received norms governing performance practices with respect to pitch, timbre, harmony, rhythm, and instrumental technique. Some improvisers, perhaps most notably pioneering British guitarist Derek Bailey, have used the term "non-idiomatic improvisation" to refer to this particular approach. "Non-idiomatic improvisation," writes Bailey, "is most usually found in so-called 'free' improvisation and, while it can be highly stylised, is not usually tied to representing an idiomatic identity."[25]

But as philosopher Gary Peters has pointed out in his book *Improvising Improvisation: From out of Philosophy, Music, Dance, and Literature,* the term "nonidiomatic" can be "a tricky one."[26] After all, what happens when musical gestures and practices that were once unconventional themselves settle into their own kind of orthodoxy? Peters references George Lewis, noting Lewis's suggestion "that the act of liberating oneself from the constraints of specific idioms, jazz in particular, might also (albeit often unwittingly) result in what Lewis describes as the 'erasure' of, in this case, an alternative black aesthetic that might challenge the often unspoken Eurocentrism of much non-idiomatic improvisation."[27]

In contrast, many improvisers working in what Lewis has described as "Afrological" improvisatory idioms have connected the quest for musical freedom with broader struggles for social and political freedom—freedom from oppression. It is perhaps worth remembering that during the 1960s at the height of the civil rights movement, many musicians referred to the new musical language being developed by Ornette Coleman, Cecil Taylor, Albert Ayler, John Coltrane, and others as "freedom music." Tenor saxophonist Archie Shepp summarizes: "This music is political by its very nature. The first music we created was a protest music that recanted slavery and spoke for liberation and freedom, and it always has."[28] For Shepp and many others, improvised modes of music making are powerful sites for challenging oppression and inspiring political action, which has profound implications for the ways in which we teach and learn improvisation, and its multiple and varied histories.

Since the 1970s, "creative music" has often served as a coded term for Afrological improvisatory forms. In a 1974 essay entitled "American Music," for example, trumpeter and Association for the Advancement of Creative Musicians (AACM) member Leo Smith distinguishes between two traditions of "art" music in America: creative music and classical music. "I use the term creative music to apply to improvised music brought alive by the creative improvisor," Smith writes, "either through reference to a score provided for his or her exploitation or through absolute improvisation; the term classical music refers to composed music brought alive by the performer through interpretation of a score."[29] Although we are inclined to raise questions about the implication that classical music is somehow less creative than modes of music making that emphasize improvisation to a greater extent, the concept of "creative music" has remained an influential one within the field of improvised music and improvised music pedagogy. For example, the Creative Music Studio was an influential center for the study of improvisation founded by Karl Berger, Ingrid Sertso, and Ornette Coleman in Woodstock, New York. Between 1971 and 1984, the Creative Music Studio brought together improvisers from jazz and various world music traditions, providing a "creative space where musicians from different backgrounds and traditions [could] explore together, share and pass on their most personal musical expression and understanding, emphasizing keen awareness, focused practice, listening and communication."[30] The emphasis on creative mobility and musical code-switching that was so integral to the Creative Music Studio's pedagogical approach resonates with the concept of "pan-idiomatic" improvisation, in which musicians are able to reference a multiplicity of musical traditions and techniques.

As these examples make clear, the language that we use to discuss and teach improvised music—on the bandstand, in our writing, or in the classroom—needs to be understood in the context of broader debates about the roles that various modes of knowledge production play in shaping understandings of public value and cultural legitimacy, and in promulgating an entire range of assumptions and value judgments about important matters such as community, identity, history, and difference. Some sense of what's at stake in these debates as they are currently playing out through music education is evident in the critical uproar that emerged in response to a keynote talk by music theorist Philip Ewell at the 2019 Society for Music Theory conference. Ewell's talk, titled "Music Theory's White Racial Frame," reflected on the institutional and structural implications of the "remarkably white" nature of the field of music theory, a whiteness that's registered not just in terms of the theorists who analyze the music, but also in terms of the artists whose work music theory has privileged. While Ewell's talk isn't about improvisation, his arguments should put us in mind of the comments from Vijay Iyer that we quoted earlier. Indeed, Ewell's critique of the white racial frame that has shaped so much of the thinking and teaching about music theory is consistent with our own sense, reinforced by Iyer's comments, that the paucity of serious institutional recognition of improvisation has been accompanied by the near erasure of subaltern perspectives from music education. We share the concerns expressed by Ewell, and we find his critique to be both timely and urgent.[31] However, it's clear that many music theorists and educators don't feel the same way. When the *Journal of Schenkerian Studies* responded by devoting almost the entirety of its twelfth volume to an eighty-nine-page rebuttal to Ewell, a Black scholar, by an apparently all-white group of scholars, it became evident that he had hit a nerve. While a detailed analysis of the critical debate that ensued is outside the scope of our analysis here, we mention this incident because it reminds us of the systemic and structural mechanisms of anti-Black racism that have shaped (and continue to influence and inflect) entire fields of inquiry, including music theory and music education. We mention it also to prompt what musicologist Jacqueline Warwick, in her consideration of the response to Ewell's critique, calls "an unflinching examination of our collective investment in the music of the past and in musical whiteness."[32] Such an examination, she admits, will "be challenging, but the boundaries can dissolve between performance and creation, classical and vernacular musics, and theory and application. Now is the time to work together, in recognition that what we teach matters."[33] The title of Warwick's essay says it all: "Music Education Has a Race Problem, and Universities Must Address It." We couldn't agree more.

Many Classrooms

"To state the obvious," as Natalie Loveless argues in her book *How to Make Art at the End of the World: A Manifesto for Research-Creation*, "how one does one's pedagogy in a field impacts what *can* and *is* done in that field."[34] She continues:

> How we train our students [and others] to think about their practices impacts how, and where, and why they move forward toward the futures they are developing. Learning environments impact the kinds of questions that can be asked, and the ways in which students are supported in asking them. As feminist, antiracist, and decolonial theorists have long taught us, pedagogical ideologies—regimes of truth—configure the parameters of legitimate research questions as well as what counts as rigor or excellence for both student and teacher. And, in turn, the ways in which internal and national granting boards understand the stakes and parameters of a field, and how these line up with that granting body's areas of interest (such as the endowment's conditions, the university's mandate, or the national granting body's target areas), has *everything* to do, in the contemporary university . . . with what kind of work is supported, therefore what kind of work is more likely to be made, seen, acclaimed, and given the chance to impact others.[35]

As Loveless's comments make clear, *what* we teach matters. So too, does *how* we teach and *why*. And as we urge a rethinking of the places where we look for knowledge, the question of *where* we teach deserves our attention. What, how, why, and where: our book opens up these questions to explore the rich and varied discourses surrounding multiple pedagogies of improvisation. In keeping with William Parker's words at the outset of this introduction, we examine a different type of "classroom" or learning environment in each chapter of this book. Chapter One may be of greatest interest to musicians who are relatively new to musical improvisation. It examines autodidactic methods of learning to improvise, including the role of influences and the development of an expanded musical vocabulary, emphasizing the dialogic dimensions of supposedly self-guided methods of learning. Chapter Two is aimed at a wider audience of students, teachers, and scholars of improvised music. It draws on interviews we conducted with improvising musicians to examine various modes of co-learning, including the role of mentorship, collaborative performances, and jam sessions within improvisatory modes of musical discourse. Chapter Three looks at the ways in which festivals can function as alternative pedagogical institutions that facilitate and promote the development of improvisatory skills, while putting critical pressure on some of the assumptions, languages, histories, and narratives too frequently promulgated by dominant pedagogical practices and institutional frameworks. In addition to musicians and scholars, this chapter will be of interest to arts workers involved in the presentation of improvisatory musics. Chapter Four examines the changing role of improvisation pedagogy within the academy and takes up the question of what happens when improvisation goes to school. Accordingly, it may be of greatest interest to educators who teach improvisation in college or university settings. Finally, in chapter five, we consider community-oriented approaches to improvisation pedagogy and the far-reaching implications of the ways that musicians are acculturated to worldviews based on improvisatory systems of musical logic, themselves expressions of community. We hope that this chapter will be of interest to students and teachers of improvisation alike, and to a broad audience of musicians, scholars, arts workers, and community activists.

Of course, none of the sites through which we learn to improvise exist in isolation. The individual, collaborative, institutional, and community-oriented dimensions of musical improvisation discussed in each of this book's chapters are interrelated in myriad ways. Improvising musicians develop within and across each of these pedagogical sites by improvising their own unique pathways among them. This book is the result of a similarly dialogic process that involves not only the two authors, but also a wide range of theoretical ideas and conversations that we have had with other educators, students, and improvisers. Indeed, the process of writing this book is not unlike that of cocreating a piece of improvised music: both activities involve the negotiation of a wide variety of ideas and voices, allowing for the emergence of something new and unforeseen. Even when it's our solo voices and lived experiences that seem to be highlighted, those voices and experiences are the product of a genuinely cocreative process.

We have deliberately adopted a flexible authorial voice, engaged in a kind of collaborative autoethnography, that shifts between first-person experiential accounts and coauthored passages that analyze a range of pedagogical experiences, sites, practices, and outcomes.[36] In this regard, our approach is similar to that of Maria Lugones and Elizabeth Spelman in their landmark essay "Have We Got a Theory for You! Feminist Theory, Cultural Imperialism and the Demand for 'the Woman's Voice.'" Like Lugones and Spelman, "We write together without presupposing unity of expression or of experience. So when we speak in unison it means just that—there are two voices and not just one."[37]

<table><tr><td>ONE</td><td>|</td><td>Solo Dialogics</td></tr></table>

ONE | Solo Dialogics

Autodidactic Methods of Learning to Improvise

Autodidacticism, the act of teaching oneself about a given subject, is an essential part of the learning process for most, if not all, musicians working in creative improvisation. "Music that is learned outside the mainstream," note Una MacGlone and Raymond MacDonald, "is . . . likely to require autodidactic strategies to a greater extent than music catered for by the educational establishment."[1] Indeed, in their qualitative assessment of learning processes of improvising musicians, MacGlone and MacDonald identify autodidactism as a key learning pathway. And as George Lewis writes in his Notes and Opinions piece in the special pedagogy issue of *Critical Studies in Improvisation / Études critiques en improvisation*, "Autodidact communities developed local variants of a practice of 'open' or 'free' improvisation that blurred the boundaries between improvisation as performance, as critical musical inquiry, and as political and social activism, all in the course of researching new sounds and modes of communication."[2]

Self-directed forms of study rarely, if ever, exist in isolation. Take, for example, the case of saxophonist Sonny Rollins. In 1959, at a time when he was arguably at the pinnacle of his career, Rollins famously stopped performing in public in order to spend long hours practicing alone on the Williamsburg Bridge between Manhattan and Brooklyn. "I was there for about two years, in summer and winter, practicing up to 14 hours a day," he remembers.[3] Rollins returned in 1962 with an album appropriately titled *The Bridge* that is often regarded as the culmination of his period of solitary improvisational exploration.

The story of Rollins's self-imposed break from public performance (the first of two such breaks throughout his long and illustrious career) has become a part of jazz lore, and is often framed by jazz historians, musicians, and enthusiasts as the ultimate example of an individual artist engaged in a meditative process of self-learning and self-discovery that enabled him to hone and perfect his craft.

Although it is seductive to interpret such intense forms of solo improvisatory practice as an expression of private, autodidactic processes of musical learning, Rollins's own remarks about the experience suggest that there is more to the story. Asked in a 2008 interview why he chose to practice on the bridge, Rollins responded, "One reason was to avoid disturbing a woman next door who was expecting a baby. But the main reason was to find a place where I could grow without worrying about anyone hearing me. Soon after I started going onto the bridge, I realized that it was an idyllic spot for me to re-discover myself as a musician. There were boats below with their horns. There were birds. It felt great to be up there under the stars."[4] Although Rollins cites as a primary impetus for his time on the bridge his desire to be alone in a place where he could engage in a process of individual musical exploration, growth, and self-discovery, he also states that he was responding to a particular social arrangement: he did not want to disturb his neighbor. His comments suggest that he was attentive to the environment around him in other ways as well: to the sound of horns, birds, and boats. Just as the quotation from William Parker with which we began this book reminds us that "the songs of birds and other sound makers who live in nature" are an inspirational part of the "classroom" of life, it is clear that Rollins's personal growth as a musician during his time on the bridge was shaped by wider spheres of influence and interaction.

There is evidence to suggest that Rollins's period of intense solo practice between 1959 and 1961 was shaped by musical influences as well. Numerous commentators have noted a shift in Rollins's playing when he returned to public performance and recording early in 1962. For example, Marc Myers suggests that "*The Bridge* is a fascinating recording and marks another turning point in Sonny's artistic development. Not only is his sound edgier and more soulful than in the past, but his improvisation is looser, faster and much more experimental."[5] We suggest that these shifts in Rollins's playing bear the influence of other improvising saxophonists including Coleman Hawkins, who had long been a major source of inspiration to Rollins; John Coltrane, who was both a close friend and previous collaborator; and perhaps even Ornette Coleman, who had famously, if controversially, made his New York City debut with an extended engagement at the Five Spot around the time that Rollins began practicing on the bridge. Asked in a 2011 interview about his decision to take a break from public performance, Rollins remembers: "I was being told by everybody: 'Oh Sonny, you the man! Don't go away. People will forget about you.' But something inside me was saying: 'No Sonny. You've got to improve man. You've got Coltrane and Ornette Coleman and these boys coming up. You've better get your stuff together.'"[6] In another interview, Rollins said of Coltrane: "His influence was pervasive. It's inevitable to have influences. Any guy who's that much into music is bound to be listening heavily to someone before them . . . like I did with Coleman Hawkins. The individuality will come out if it's there. It depends whether the player can transcend the influence. To play what we call modern music, you'd have to have some antecedents."[7] Listening to *The Bridge* and recordings of performances from the period, it is clear that Rollins both absorbed and transcended a wide variety of musical antecedents, including the influence of his mentor (Hawkins) and friend (Coltrane).

Another notable shift in Rollins's playing after his time on the bridge was the introduction of extended, stream-of-consciousness-like solo improvisations—both with and without accompaniment—in which he would quote from a wide range of musical sources, including not only jazz standards, but also popular and folk melodies and even nursery rhymes—all woven together in a seamless web of improvisatory musical expression. Recorded at a concert in the sculpture garden of New York's Museum of Modern Art, Rollins's 1985 recording simply titled *The Solo Album* provides an interesting (if considerably later) example of Rollins's approach to solo improvisation. On it, he wends his way through a wide variety of rhythmic and melodic ideas, incorporating fleeting melodic fragments from such diverse sources as "Ornithology," "Mairzy Doats," "The Nearness of You," "Jim," "Home! Sweet Home!," "Pop Goes the Weasel," and his own compositions "St. Thomas" and "Everywhere Calypso."

Even solo improvisatory acts, such as Rollins's lengthy postbridge improvisations, are in constant dialogue with a multiplicity of musical influences and sources. In his book *Group Genius: The Creative Power of Collaboration*, psychologist Keith Sawyer suggests "that the mind itself is filled with a kind of collaboration, that even the insights that emerge when you're completely alone can be traced back to previous collaborations."[8] Thus, we are tempted to regard the title of Rollins's comeback album not just as an homage to the bridge itself, nor even to the hundreds of hours that he spent there improvising, learning, and honing his craft, but rather as a reflection of the metaphorical bridges between Rollins and the myriad of musical influences that animate his remarkable improvisatory practice, as well as the wider patterns of lived experience that informed and shaped his musical development.[9]

Clearly, we are never really alone when we practice on our own. As literary theorist Mikhail Bakhtin explains, "Life by its very nature is dialogic. To live means to participate in dialogue: to ask questions, to heed, to respond, to agree, and so forth. In this dialogue a person participates wholly and throughout his [*sic*] whole life: with his eyes, lips, hands, soul, spirit, with his whole body and deeds. He invests his entire self in discourse, and this discourse enters into the dialogic fabric of human life, into the world symposium."[10] Learning to improvise also means "to participate in dialogue: to ask questions, to heed, to respond, to agree" and, we would add, to disagree. In this view, Bakhtin's thought-provoking reference to "the world symposium" resonates with bassist William Parker's insight that there are many classrooms: both ideas suggest that all of our life experiences influence our development as people and, by extension, as improvisers.

Among the life experiences that influence our approach to improvisation are the patterns of socialization through which we learn how to interact with others, especially those who are different from us; how we are taught to deal with unforeseen (and *unforeheard*) ideas and circumstances; as well as the stories that we are told, and learn to tell, through words, through actions, and through music. As Nigerian poet and novelist Ben Okri suggests, "We live by stories, we also live in them. One way or another we are living the stories planted in us early or along the way, or we are also living the stories we planted—knowingly or unknowingly—in ourselves."[11] What kind of stories do we live by and in—and teach and learn—in life's many classrooms, and how do they influence the music that we make?

Just as oral and written stories depend on language, the musical stories that we learn to tell depend on the acquisition and development of a flexible and generative musical language that we can draw upon and modify in the course of performance.[12] As Theodor Adorno notes, "Music is similar to language in that it is a temporal succession of articulated sounds that are more than just sound. They say something, often something humane."[13] Although some of Adorno's other writings suggest that his conception of "humane music" was quite different from our own, we agree with his notion that all languages, including musical ones, rely on vocabularies, syntaxes, and grammars that shape the ways in which sounds are organized and meanings are produced. In *Improvisation: Its Nature and Practice in Music*, improvising guitarist Derek Bailey elaborates on the analogy between language and improvised music:

> The analogy with language, often used by improvising musicians in discussing their work, has a certain usefulness in illustrating the development of a common stock of material—a vocabulary—which takes place when a group of musicians improvise together regularly. With a successful improvising group the bulk of their material will be initially provided by the styles, techniques and habits of the musicians involved. This vocabulary will then be developed by the musicians individually, in work and research away from the group, and collectively in performance.[14]

Following Bailey, our discussion of autodidactic methods of learning to improvise considers the ways in which improvisers acquire and develop a musical vocabulary that is both shared and personal. In doing so, we are mindful of Adorno's warning: "The person who takes music literally as language will be led astray by it."[15] Therefore, we do not equate music and language in the literal sense, but rather regard language as a fruitful metaphor for thinking through some of the ways in which we learn to improvise.

Learning the Language(s) of Improvised Music

One of the things that has characterized free improvisation over the past half century or so is its emphasis on innovation and inventiveness.[16] In *Improvisation as Art*, Edgar Landgraf suggests that inventiveness is central to improvisation in/as modern art. He explains:

> Improvisation in art not only has to be recognizable, it also has to be recognizably *inventive*, that is, recognizably different from the known and predictable. Thus the known and predictable come to serve as a foil against which the performance can alone define itself as inventive. For artist and audience alike, then, the known and predictable define the conceptual horizon that limits and simultaneously enables the recognition of inventiveness in improvisation. It is in this sense that an improvised performance is always already *mediated* by the (cultural) knowledge that limits the space of its possibility.[17]

The emphasis on inventiveness that characterizes much of the field of improvised music is particularly evident in the range of instrumental and vocal techniques that constitute the musical vocabularies of contemporary improvisers. Indeed, the use of extended techniques has become common on many instruments within the field of improvised music over the past fifty years. With the abstraction and eventual dissolution of metric and harmonic regularity in the music of Cecil Taylor, Ornette Coleman, Derek Bailey, and subsequent generations of improvising musicians since the 1950s and 1960s, improvisers have explored the timbral possibilities of voices and instruments in new ways. Improvising pianists have used hands, fists, and forearms to create dense tone clusters; reed players have explored circular breathing and multiphonic techniques; and percussionists have investigated new and unorthodox ways of generating percussive sound.[18]

The emphasis on inventiveness within improvisatory musical discourse is evident even in the use of the adjective "free" when referring to improvised modes of music making, as in "free jazz," "free improvisation," or simply "free music." To a significant extent, conceptions of improvisatory musical freedom have been articulated through the use of expanded—and expanding—musical vocabularies. However, extended musical vocabularies are never entirely unique to individual improvisers. Indeed, a significant portion of an improviser's musical vocabulary is shared with, or at least informed by, that of other improvising musicians, especially the ones he or she has listened to and learned from. As improvising saxophonist Steve Lacy put it, "Each player who comes along affects the common pool of language. When you hear a new player— and you make it your business to hear anyone who comes along and has something new—then you have to go back and rethink everything."[19]

Audio (and, increasingly, video) recordings are an important avenue through which improvisers encounter musicians who "have something new." Writing specifically about the context of jazz pedagogy, David Ake has made the point that "no pedagogical tool has left as widespread or as long-lasting an impact on jazz skill acquisition as have the various media of sound recording. Records, tapes, and CDs not only act," he tells us, "as the physical 'texts' of jazz, they also serve as the pre-eminent 'text-books' of the music, providing study materials for all players."[20] Furthermore, Ake suggests that "records (and also radio broadcasts) can cross racial, national and other boundaries in a way that people often cannot (or will not). That is, individuals who would otherwise have no access to cultures different from their own can experience alternative possibilities of music-making."[21]

What may be the case for jazz skill acquisition may not apply as readily to the pedagogy of improvisation. After all, knowledge of—and access to—audio and video recordings of improvised music continues to be restricted by a network of commercial forces and cultural gatekeepers that privilege certain forms of music (generally those that are the most profitable) at the expense of modes of music making that have been rendered less profitable, often by those very same forces. Most forms of improvised music fall into the latter category.

Nonetheless, the acts of listening to, studying, and playing along with recordings of improvised music are a crucial part of most improvisers' musical development. For instance, pioneering British saxophonist Evan Parker told us how, when he started playing, he learned primarily from recordings:

> I started playing at the age of fourteen wanting to play like Paul Desmond. Gradually my musical researches led me to John Coltrane and I wanted to play like him. I switched from alto to soprano and tenor. . . . I was also listening to records and tried to assimilate the implications of what was at that point an art form in a rapid phase of development.[22]

For improvising musicians today, virtually the entire history of recorded sound is available for study through a few strokes on a computer keyboard.

As we will discuss in chapters three and four, arts presenters and educators can play a vital role in challenging dominant frameworks surrounding cultural production by exposing listeners to musical ideas, recordings, and resources that they are not likely to encounter otherwise. As a means to that end, we have compiled a partial discography of improvised music that is meant to function as a complement to the discography of improvised music compiled by George Lewis for his 1996 essay "Improvised Music after 1950." Although neither list is exhaustive, when taken together, they provide a thorough introduction to the recorded histories of free improvisation, pan-idiomatic improvisation, and creative improvised music to date. We recommend that students of improvised music spend time learning from these recordings and other recordings by the improvising musicians represented in the discography.

In addition to learning from audio and video recordings of other improvising musicians, listening to audio recordings of one's own improvisations can be a powerful form of self-learning. Over time, many improvisers develop musical habits that become so deeply ingrained within their musical vocabularies that they are unaware of the extent to which they rely on them in performance. For example, many inexperienced jazz drummers have a tendency to accent "beat 1" on the bass drum every four or eight measures when they are playing music with a recursive rhythmic and harmonic structure, subconsciously signposting the structure of the music. This practice often has the effect of stunting the flow of musical time and the phrasing of soloists. Similarly, musicians working in other modes of improvised music can develop musical habits that they use—and overuse—without necessarily knowing that they are doing so. Listening to recordings of our own solo and group improvisations can serve as a self-diagnostic tool that enables us to identify such musical habits and develop musical alternatives.

Along with learning from recordings of improvised music, experiencing live musical performances can provide valuable learning experiences that allow us not only to hear, but also to see how other improvisers produce particular kinds of sounds on their instruments. This can be especially helpful for learning so-called extended techniques that characterize the musical language(s) associated with the field of contemporary improvised music. For example, I (Jesse) learned a great deal from a solo performance by percussionist Gerry Hemingway at the 1996 edition of the Guelph Jazz Festival. Hemingway used a wide variety of extended techniques on the drum set to create innovative and compelling sound worlds that came as a revelation to me. I had heard many of these techniques on recordings, but in some cases, I was unable to intuit the performative techniques and gestures involved in their production from audio recordings alone. Seeing Gerry use those techniques in performance opened my eyes and ears to many additional possibilities on the drum set.

That encounter was a valuable learning experience for me, and one that points to some of the other pedagogical models and sites discussed in subsequent chapters including the role of mentors and musical collaborators (chapter two), and the importance of music festivals as sites for the transmission of musical knowledge (chapter three). After seeing and hearing Gerry perform, I began exploring some of the techniques that I had seen him use. However, it was important to me that I not simply imitate his musical vocabulary. Rather, I worked to understand some of the generative principles underlying his performance practice so that I could incorporate those principles into my own developing musical vocabulary, using them in my own way. This "imitate to innovate" process represents another important aspect of learning the art of improvisation, one that is accomplished largely through solo practice.

When I (Ajay) reflect on how I learned to improvise as a musician, I too recognize that I was largely self-taught. But, as per our arguments throughout this chapter, I also realize that I was never really alone as I learned. Although I had received some formal musical training on the piano from a young age, other moments now stand out to me as being much more formative. For one thing, I grew up in a musical household. My father was a classical Indian musician (a sitarist and vocalist). He studied classical Indian vocal music for several years under the tutelage of Pundit Modi, an expert of the Gwalior and Agra gharanas of Hindustani music. He also studied sitar in Mumbai with P. G. Parab. He had a deep knowledge of the music and knew many rare ragas. After my father's retirement as a professor of mathematics from the University of Toronto, he began teaching classical Indian (vocal and sitar) music from his home to Toronto-area residents on a volunteer basis. I grew up attending concerts with my father and being exposed to recordings of the music. And throughout the seventies, I fondly recall many exciting musical evenings taking place at our home in Toronto (house concerts as they are called now), where amazing artists (including my dad and many of his friends) would perform for our community late into the night. I remember, too, my father and mother organizing and hosting concerts by world-class musicians such as tabla virtuoso Pandit Nikhil Ghosh at our house. I remember other famous musicians, such as the great Indian playback singer Lata Mangeshkar, once known to have been the most recorded artist in music history, passing through our house. At the time that these wonderful events were happening and these remarkable people were passing through our lives, I don't remember much fuss being made about them. It seemed, at least at the time, as though they were just an ordinary part of a vibrant cultural community. When I think back on these times now, I realize how truly extraordinary these memories are, and how they have played a role in shaping so many of my own commitments and priorities to teaching, learning, and community.

Another formative moment in my learning as an improviser came about when I had the opportunity to study composition with Dr. Philip McConnell in high school. Although Dr. McConnell's classes weren't focused on improvisation, they did stretch my ears and expand my awareness of musical possibilities, much like the music to which I was exposed through my father. In fact, the elements of musical composition that I learned from Dr. McConnell's class played a key role in many of my own musical ventures during that highly creative period of my life, informing the music I was composing and performing with various experimental rock, electronic, and jazz-based groups. One of those groups I played with in the early eighties featured, among others, saxophonist Richard Underhill (who would go on to become a founding member of the jazz-funk-fusion group Shuffle Demons) and clarinetist Don McKellar (now best known as an actor, writer, and film director). Although the group's repertoire consisted of composed pieces, we often found ourselves experimenting with long stretches of largely free-form improvisation. In short, when it comes to improvisation, I've learned largely by doing.

At the time that I was studying composition with Dr. McConnell, I was also heavily inspired and influenced by the music I was listening to on recordings. Looking back on the most salient factors that contributed to my development as an improvising musician, I'm tempted to cite as another formative pedagogical moment the time I went to my favorite record shop in Toronto, Records on Wheels, seeking to trade in my Paul McCartney and Wings LPs for recordings by Karlheinz Stockhausen. Unfortunately, there were no Stockhausen recordings in stock, but the staff at the record store happily directed me to the album *Opener* by the pioneering experimental German rock group Can, which developed its material largely through a process of spontaneous composition. To this day, much of my own improvising continues to be influenced by the music I was first exposed to through that recording. In retrospect, it is clear that for me, like so many other improvisers, listening was a key part of my process of learning to improvise. My transformative experience with Can suggests that one of the most vital things that recordings enable, to quote again from David Ake, is the opportunity to "experience alternative possibilities of music-making."[23]

It is important to note the role that the staff at the record store played in facilitating my exposure to these alternative musical possibilities: it was thanks to their knowledge, and their role as arbiters of musical taste, that I first discovered the paradigm-shifting music of Can.[24] For several generations of musicians, record stores have functioned as important sites for learning and knowledge exchange. The dominance of digital music distribution has changed the way that many musicians discover new modes of music making, at times limiting their exposure to musical ideas that lie outside normative popular music models. As physical record stores have waned in number, the other pedagogical sites that we discuss later in this book (bandstands, classrooms, music festivals, etc.) have assumed even greater importance in exposing musicians, and the listening public more generally, to alternative possibilities of music making.[25]

Practicing Improvisation to Learn Improvisation Practice

There is considerable debate among improvisers about the merits of practicing one's instrument. Some improvisers suggest that practicing, at least as it is traditionally understood, is unnecessary—perhaps even antithetical—to free improvisation. In particular, numerous improvisers have questioned the emphasis on technical mastery over one's instrument that seems to be the aim of many forms of musical practice. For example, toward the end of her long and distinguished career, improvising accordionist Pauline Oliveros told us that she no longer practiced her instrument in the traditional sense, having instead cultivated a philosophy and practice that she referred to as "deep listening," which informed her approach to improvisation and, indeed, all of her work:

> At this stage of my improvisations, I don't practice. At least I am not striving to master my instrument. That kind of practice that embeds patterns or techniques is not what I need or want. I want my improvisations to be free of old patterns and full of fresh ideas that come from a deeper unknown strata of my psyche. What I do practice is listening to everything all the time as much as I possibly can. I feel that it is important to play the world as I hear it, no matter what, spontaneously.[26]

Pauline's comments about playing the world as she hears it point once again to the wider spheres of lived experience—the "many classrooms" and "world symposium"—that inform the ways in which we learn to improvise. In a sense, by listening as attentively as possible to the world around her, Pauline was practicing—and learning—all the time. Rather than strive to master her instrument in a conventional way, she learned, through her practice of deep listening, to engage in music making that is genuinely open, and receptive, to everything that is around her when she improvises. In short, she learned (and spent much of her career showing others) that music is everywhere, all around us, all the time.

For some musicians, particularly those who are steeped in musical traditions in which improvisation does not necessarily play a major role, learning to improvise can be a process of "unlearning," a letting go of previous musical habits or at least a critical reexamination of those habits. For example, Korean percussionist Dong-Won Kim came to free improvisation from a musical background that is deeply rooted in the traditional musics of Korea. He describes his approach to free improvisation as a process of "dismantling" his previous musical habits:

> For me, improvising is the best way to open my heart to others, and the ultimate expression of being flexible musically. To achieve this goal, I believe that I shouldn't be repeating my previous habits, practices, and vocabularies in my favorite way. In order to achieve that level of decent improvisation, I believe that I have to dismantle my previous habits. By giving up my favorite things, I can listen much more carefully to others, and be more responsive to others.[27]

He is quick to point out that this process of musical dismantling through improvisation does not undermine his musical or cultural identity. Indeed, he describes Korean traditional music as an indelible part of his musical identity, likening it to the genetic building blocks of life. "I believe that real creation always comes from the level of DNA," he stresses, "not from superficiality."[28] Therefore, he is not concerned about trying to imbue his free improvisations with signifiers of traditional Korean music; his identity as a Korean musician and storyteller is always already inscribed within every note he plays.

Clarinetist François Houle describes the development and expression of his own personal language as involving a process that evolved from "drawing elements from a multitude of musical sources: classical, contemporary new music, jazz, world traditions, and experimental electroacoustic music."[29] Like Dong-Won Kim, Houle acknowledges that a process of undoing has been central to his self-learning and his identity as an improvising musician: "Rather than transcribing and lifting patterns and solo ideas from the jazz canon," he explains, "I was more drawn to the idiosyncratic tendencies of my major influences as a point of departure. I had to undo a lot of my practicing habits in order to restructure my awareness towards fundamental musical parameters, which to me seemed vital to understanding sound as learning from an established theoretical treatise."[30]

As important as processes of "unlearning" are to many improvisers' musical development, most improvising musicians do spend time practicing their instrument(s) and honing their skills. Derek Bailey identifies three interrelated types of solo practice among improvisers: technical practice, exercises designed to help us learn new musical material, and "woodshedding."[31] He describes technical practice as "the musical equivalent of running on the spot"—musical practice aimed at maintaining one's "chops" and keeping fit musically.[32] Technical practice might include such things as sustaining long tones in the case of performers of wind instruments, finger dexterity exercises for horn players, guitarists, and pianists, scales and arpeggios for performers of pitched instruments, single- and double-stroke rolls for percussionists, and so on. Many improvisers seem to agree that technical proficiency is useful insofar as it allows us to realize our musical ideas. In most cases, a greater range of musical techniques will enable an improviser to realize a greater range of musical ideas and enter into improvisatory dialogue with improvisers coming from a wider variety of musical backgrounds.

As an improviser's vocabulary expands, so too will the range of technical exercises that he or she practices. For example, improvising baritone saxophonist David Mott undertakes a rigorous regiment of physical training in order to perform some of the extended techniques that he uses in performance. He explains:

> I have to build up the arm and finger musculature to be able to sustain the repetition as long as I'd like, while also developing the lung capacity (for circular breathing on the baritone) and the energy to maintain it over a length of time. So I have to go into a training mode, like preparing to run a marathon, in order to build the endurance necessary to sustain the techniques. While I have a general level of endurance that I maintain, some of my "comprovisations" require a special effort.[33]

Mott is also cautious to avoid repetitive strain injuries caused by this type of practice. "I'm wary of pushing my body to do this all the time and so have managed to avoid difficulties like tendonitis," he explains. "Running a car flat out over time is not the best idea if you want it to last."[34]

The second type of solo practice identified by Bailey "is centred on exercises worked out to deal specifically with the manipulative demands made by new material."[35] New musical material can come from a variety of sources. As George Lewis suggests, "Individual improvisers are now able to reference an intercultural establishment of techniques, styles, aesthetic attitudes, antecedents, and networks of cultural and social practice."[36] For improvisers whose performance practice incorporates elements of jazz, popular musics, and non-Western musical traditions, this might entail practicing particular musical materials (scales, rhythms, playing techniques) that are associated with those traditions. In addition, many improvisers practice extended techniques with a view of internalizing those techniques to the point that they are able to draw on them during the course of performance. This is an important way of developing one's personal musical voice, albeit one that is informed by—and in dialogue with—the work of other improvisers.

Some improvisers go about the process of extending their musical vocabularies in a more or less organic way through a process of experimentation on their instruments. Quoting again from David Mott:

> There are two means by which most of the extended techniques I use came (and continue to come) about. The first is by spending time on the horn, trying this and trying that to see what I can find. Like, what happens if I lift this finger (creating an unorthodox fingering)? Now can I split a tone with different kinds of pressure with my embouchure using that fingering? Etc. Sometimes lucky accidents occur which I note and then explore. The other is by imagining either sounds or techniques and then going back to the horn to see if I can find a means of realizing what I imagined. In all cases, when a technique is difficult, I would spend only five minutes a day working with it. This is how I taught myself circular breathing, for example (having heard and seen both Harry Carney and Rahsaan Roland Kirk use it), taking a year until I felt comfortable enough to use it in public.[37]

In addition to highlighting the dialogic nature of learning to improvise, Mott's comments emphasize the importance of experimentation and imagination—trying different things out on one's instrument, but also imagining new sonic possibilities and then trying to bring them into existence. In many ways, experimentation and imagination are the twin pillars of both practicing improvisation and improvisational practice. The history of improvised music is filled with musicians who have experimented musically in order to imagine new musical and social possibilities: from Sun Ra to Anthony Braxton, from Jeanne Lee to Joëlle Léandre, from Derek Bailey to William Parker.

Some improvisers approach the development of an expanded musical vocabulary in a highly systematic way. For example, early in his career, multi-instrumentalist Anthony Braxton developed and codified a series of sound classifications. Interestingly, he refers to these different types of sounds as "language types."[38] Each of these language types, which include such groupings as "smeared sounds," "spiral sounds," and "intervallic formings," is represented visually by a particular line drawing. Taken together, these language types constitute much of Braxton's vocabulary as both an improviser and composer.

Likewise, I (Jesse) tried to be somewhat methodical in my approach to developing an extended musical vocabulary as an improvising percussionist. Early in my career, I developed the loose conceptual framework for thinking about percussive sound. I came to realize that there are essentially two types of percussive sounds: those that are sustainable, and those that are more or less discrete. By sustainable, I mean those sounds that can continue without interruption as long as the performative action is carried out. In contrast, discrete sound events cannot be sustained continuously but are instead the result of a single physical gesture. To borrow an analogy from the visual realm, a discrete sound can be likened to a point while a sustainable sound is like a line. These types of percussive sounds constitute the extreme ends of a continuum: discrete sounds may give the illusion of uninterruptedness if they are played in rapid succession. To extend the analogy with visual perception, a sustained sound can be compared to a continuous, unbroken line, while a single- or double-stroke roll can be compared with a broken or dotted line.

Each of these sound types, sustainable and discrete, can be further broken down into several subcategories of percussive sound. Sustainable sounds include those that depend on friction for their production such as bowed cymbals, and various types of rubs and scrapes (with brushes, hands, metal, etc.). In addition, rolls of various types can be sustained: each individual articulation is generally subsumed by the wash of sound that results. Other percussion instruments that yield sustainable sounds include various kinds of shakers and rattles.

Discrete percussive sounds, on the other hand, break down into two general categories: those with a short attack and short decay and those with a short attack and a relatively long decay. The difference between the two depends on the nature of the material being struck. Group A discrete sounds (that is, those with a short attack and short decay) are generally elicited from one of three drum set surfaces: drum membranes, metal hardware (cymbal and drum stands, for example), and wood, fiberglass, or metal drum shells. The high hat is a special case because it has some variability in terms of its sound envelope: bringing the upper and lower high-hat cymbals firmly together with the foot-operated mechanism yields a Group A discrete sound event, as does the practice of striking a pair of tightly closed high-hat cymbals with a stick or mallet. However, striking an open high-hat cymbal will result in a long decay time after the initial attack, as will the practice of bringing the high-hat cymbals together and quickly releasing them ("splashing" the high-hat cymbals, in drummer parlance). Similarly, the practice of "choking" a ride or crash cymbal yields a Group A sound, while cymbals that are left to vibrate freely without dampening generally result in Group B sound events.

When I first ventured into the realm of free improvisation, I was overwhelmed—as many novice improvisers are—by the number of musical options that were available to me. Like Braxton's "language types," my typology of drum set sounds helped me make sense of my expanding musical vocabulary and provided a framework within which I could experiment musically and explore variations in the new sounds that I was discovering. I realized that all of the percussive sounds in my emergent musical vocabulary could be varied in virtually any musical parameter. Although rhythm has historically been the musical parameter most closely associated with percussion (and the one that receives the greatest amount of attention in drum set literature and pedagogy), percussive sounds can be varied in other parameters too, including intensity or loudness, temporal density, timbre, and pitch. For improvisers on any instrument, variation is an essential tool for expanding one's musical vocabulary and an essential part of autodidactic methods of learning to improvise.

Whether improvisers expand their musical vocabularies through an intuitive process of musical experimentation or in a more systematic manner, it is important that they absorb their new musical language to the point that they don't necessarily have to think about its constituent elements in the course of performance, but can instead become deeply immersed in the musical moment, entering into what psychologist Mihaly Csikszentmihalyi famously termed a state of *flow*, "the state in which people are so involved in an activity that nothing else seems to matter."[39] Improvisers must be able to put together elements of their musical vocabularies more or less instantaneously in order to make a musical statement that is appropriate and meaningful within the context in which it is made. For most improvisers, this level of spontaneous fluency is achieved through years of practicing their instruments.

William Parker puts it this way: "I don't practice what I am going to play on the bass. I meditate and practice how to flow with fire if the music ignites to a level larger than itself." He continues:

> The notes, melodies, or rhythms have already been heavily digested;
> they are like sleeping cells waiting to be woken up; they are embryos
> waiting to be born and take a life of their own. I have to practice not
> interfering with the music. Rather flow with it, dance with it. Knowing
> when to follow and knowing when to lead. The goal is to train your
> senses to allow sound to live free rather than impose musical devices
> on it.[40]

On one hand, Parker states that he does not practice what he is going to
play in performance, thereby avoiding the trap of relying on memorized
patterns—what he terms "musical devices"—in performance. But he
also emphasizes the importance of thoroughly absorbing or "digesting"
the notes, melodies, and rhythms that constitute one's musical vocabulary so that those things can "take a life of their own" in performance.
This comment is very much in keeping with Aaron Berkowitz's views of
the neuroscientific basis of learning to improvise. "The ability to improvise in a style relies on an intimate knowledge of the musical elements,
processes, and forms of that style," Berkowitz explains. "However, the
temporal and physical constraints of improvised performance allow little
or no room for recourse to theoretical musings about such knowledge.
The knowledge must be internalized, mentally and physically, if spontaneous fluency is to be achieved."[41]

One way to assimilate and consolidate our expanding musical vocabulary is through the third type of practice identified by Bailey, namely
"woodshedding." Bailey sees woodshedding as "the bridge between
technical practise and improvisation."[42] The term "woodshedding" has
been widely used among jazz musicians historically to refer to time spent
practicing in isolation in order to develop their improvisatory abilities
to the fullest extent possible. Think again of Sonny Rollins spending
long hours practicing on the Williamsburg Bridge. To cite another well-
known example from jazz history, think of Charlie Parker spending the
summer of 1937 woodshedding in the Ozarks, practicing in isolation to
develop and hone his craft. Just as a woodshed is a place to store wood
that will be used as fuel for fire, woodshedding refers to a type of solo
practice through which we gather, store, and refine musical ideas that
we will use in the future to fuel our improvisatory creative practice. We
might play in much the same way as we would in a performance situation, but our focus is different: we tend to be more analytical, more
aware of the details of our own playing rather than the totality of the

musical experience. We are free to try things out, to put different elements of our musical vocabulary together in different ways. We are also free to make mistakes and, crucially, to learn from those mistakes. The woodshed, then, is a space of disciplined musical experimentation and development through which we gain the knowledge, skills, and confidence necessary to bring our musical vocabulary into dialogue with that of others.

While it might be tempting to romanticize the woodshed as a place for solitary practicing and honing of skills, we would note again that our practice routines are informed by many influences that we explore through an ongoing process of sonic investigation and creative expression. We note, too, that the idea of woodshedding is often connected to gendered notions of technical "mastery." While plenty of women improvisers engage in forms of solo practice that might be described as woodshedding, some adopt a more communal approach. For example, in the late 1970s, Pauline Oliveros practiced her series of "Sonic Meditations" with a group of women in San Diego that eventually became known as the ♀ Ensemble. Think, too, of the communal practice of the Feminist Improvising Group, where the collective was more important than the individual mastery of skill. Such examples suggest that the processes through which we learn to improvise are gendered in particular ways

Clearly, the ways in which musicians learn to improvise and how they go about honing their skills vary significantly between one improviser and another, and between different social, cultural, and institutional contexts. There's one thing, though, that emerges as a common thread, namely the importance of developing an individual approach to improvisation. George Lewis notes that "'improvisations' that appear to consist mainly of unquestioning, rote regurgitation of prepared patterns are viewed by many improvisers as failing to display the kind of independent creative investigation and spontaneous invention that can lead to the discovery of what jazz musicians often call 'one's own sound,' or the original creation of one's own musical material and lexicon."[43] In general, self-learning practices, including those we've considered here, are central to the development of an improviser's own sound. An improvising musician's lexicon is further developed and honed through the processes of co-learning and cocreation that will form the basis of our inquiry and discussion in the following chapter.

Hearing What the Other Has to Play

Co-learning through Musical Improvisation

Damien Chazelle's critically acclaimed 2014 film *Whiplash* tells the fictitious story of an aspiring jazz drummer named Andrew Neiman who is studying at a prestigious music school in New York City under the tutelage of a sadistic bandleader known as Fletcher. Throughout the film, Fletcher becomes progressively more abusive toward Neiman in an effort, we are told, to elicit musical greatness from the student. Although *Whiplash* is a compelling film in many ways, its depiction of jazz and improvisation pedagogy bears little resemblance to our own experiences, or those of the vast majority of musicians we have interviewed and with whom we have collaborated. For one thing, the musicians in the film are rarely shown interacting with, or learning from, one another. This is profoundly at odds with our own experience and understanding of improvisation pedagogy, which depends vitally on various forms of dialogue and co-learning.

At one point in the film, Fletcher explains his pedagogical approach to Neiman by telling an embellished version of a mythic story about Charlie Parker who, at the age of sixteen, was humiliated by drummer Jo Jones during a jam session in Kansas City. That moment of public embarrassment, the story goes, sent Parker back to the woodshed to practice obsessively until he was able to return to the bandstand a year later having attained an astonishing level of musical virtuosity.[1] Unfortunately, this romanticized narrative only tells part of the story of Parker's learning process. In his *New Yorker* review of *Whiplash*, film critic Richard Brody explains,

Here's what Parker didn't do in the intervening year: sit alone in his room and work on making his fingers go faster. He played music, thought music, lived music. In "Whiplash," the young musicians don't play much music. Andrew isn't in a band or a combo, doesn't get together with his fellow-students and jam—not in a park, not in a subway station, not in a café, not even in a basement. He doesn't study music theory, not alone and not (as Parker did) with his peers.[2]

The peer-to-peer learning that Brody identifies as being central to Parker's musical development—and entirely absent from *Whiplash*—has remained an integral part of the co-learning processes associated with jazz and improvisation more broadly. Likewise, most forms of mentorship within the field of improvised music bear little resemblance to the abusive power dynamics shown in *Whiplash*. Rather, improviser-mentors, including those discussed in this chapter, tend to emphasize listening, mutual respect, and cocreative dialogue as central to an improvising musician's development.

In this chapter, we take a look at various processes of co-learning that shape our development as improvisers, including formative encounters with improvisation in everyday life, the role of mentorship, peer-to-peer collaboration, and jam sessions. Given that our focus here is on learning not only from—but with—one another in a spirit of cocreative discovery, and that our emphasis is on models of learning that are predicated on dialogue, we've chosen to take our cue from a series of interviews that we have conducted with improvising musicians who represent a cross section of different approaches to improvisational practice. Through these interviews, we have extended our own dialogic and cocreative process of authorship in an effort to engage in dialogue with a broader group of improvising artists with whom we've collaborated in various capacities: by presenting them at music festivals, by performing and/or recording with them, or by collaborating with them on research projects such as this one.[3]

Improvisational Pedagogies of Everyday Life

Many of the improvisers we interviewed pointed out that learning to improvise musically is fundamentally linked with processes through which we learn to improvise in everyday life. As Hamid Drake puts it, "Improvising is something we all do every day. For instance, when we have conversations, we are ad libbing and responding off of one another.

The words we use—the tone and inflection—all are unique expressions of our collective voice." He continues: "For me improvisation comes from listening and learning . . . being open to the boundless expressions. The next step is the most challenging—getting out of the way to allow what has been learned to follow its own path and flow free."[4]

When I (Ajay) asked multi-instrumentalist and Association for the Advancement of Creative Musicians member Douglas Ewart in a public interview during the 2015 Guelph Jazz Festival Colloquium about how he learned to improvise, he too stressed the importance of improvisation as part of the practice of everyday life:

> As kids, growing up in Jamaica, I came from a very rich family in terms of people that cared for you, great foods, readers, people with great integrity, people with skills and more. But we didn't have a lot of money, so—and my grandmother was a woman that was very skeptical about buying you everything that was around, particularly toys. She would always show you how it wouldn't last long, and she wasn't going to spend her money on that, and that you should make your own things. And of course, at that time, you're thinking, wow, that's kind of wicked. [Laughs] And I'm so glad she was wicked, because . . . most kids made their own toys: we made tops, we made kites, we made bats and balls, we made scooters, and we made cars. At that time, oil came in cans, and we'd cut up the cans and make the hood and the fenders and get bicycle tools and make frills and all kinds of decorative and functional things for our creations.
>
> So creativity and improvisation were endemic to our childhood. We didn't buy new nails—you might get a few new nails if somebody was constructing something and you'd go and ask a carpenter for a few nails. But we'd walk around, find old, bent nails—the ones they had pulled out of a construction—learn how to straighten them, and then learn how to drive them into a piece of wood without bending them again, which took a certain kind of subtlety in hammering.
>
> So right away, that's improvising at its height. And so improvisation for me, didn't start in the musical way, but in the process of construction. And in a way, when you make your own things, you tend to become good at figuring things out . . . how to improvise.[5]

In discussing how he came to his role as an improvising musician, Ewart chooses to speak not about music making, but rather about the art of toy making, about "learning how to make things." Ewart's contention that "this is just life, it's just what you do," is akin to Drake's claim that "improvising is something we all do every day."

Several things are worthy of our attention here. Even when they are talking about learning how to improvise musically, musicians will often move the conversation away from music making to lessons learned from the practice of everyday life. Ewart's story about how he became "good at figuring things out," how he learned to make things with the tools and resources that were available to him as a child growing up in Jamaica, reminds us that there is a vital history of improvisers who have found creative ways to respond to the life circumstances in which they have found themselves, and to make do with the materials at hand. This pattern of ingenuity and resourcefulness reinforces the notion that musical practices in which improvisation figures prominently ought to be understood as vital *social* practices. Scholars Michelle Kisliuk and Kelly Gross have put it this way:

> First-hand, embodied experience that students have with music and dance can facilitate an understanding, or at least an awareness, of both macro- and micropolitics. In learning to dance and sing in new ways, one becomes vitally aware of issues of self and other, and of "here" and "there," challenging the distancing that takes place in much disembodied scholarship. Direct involvement in a process of musical creation engenders a kind of self-awareness that leads to activity instead of abstraction.[6]

If Kisliuk and Gross are correct in suggesting that this vital awareness of self and other can lead to activity and action, then George Lewis's comments that "improvisative discourses disclose the extent to which musicians have a vital stake in the ongoing dialogue concerning the future of our planet" come into sharp relief. "Music," he continues, "becomes a necessity for existence, rather than merely a pleasant way to pass time."[7]

Lewis made a related point in his interview with us for this book: "I've probably said somewhere that one doesn't 'learn' to improvise—or rather, that what people do as musical improvisors can be regarded as one domain among many quotidian activities of improvisation, both in and out of the arts."[8] For Lewis, like Drake, Ewart, and many others, it's important to note that "we also 'learn' how to improvise in nonartistic settings, and there is also a kind of pedagogy and mentorship around that, from which musical scholars could learn a great deal. More general experiences of temporality, contingency, agency, indeterminacy, analysis of conditions, and choice in everyday human life become the basis on which we 'learn' to improvise music."[9] Pianist and scholar Vijay Iyer is similarly forthright on this point. "Life," he writes, "is a sustained improvisational interaction with the structures of the world, of the body, of culture."[10]

If the choices we make in everyday life form at least part of the basis through which we develop as improvising musicians, part of what's at issue, again in Lewis's words, is that "every encounter for which you foreground listening is an opportunity to transform your understanding of the situation into a mentorial one, where you receive instruction from both the people and the situation."[11] He elaborates: "We can view improvisation of all kinds as a kind of pedagogical relation, in which we listen to know where we are and where the others are; where ideas and information are communicated from each to the other; where one learns about the other through hearing what the other has to play; and where one learns about oneself through listening to the responses from the other that seem somehow to be related to you."[12] Listening to know, knowing to listen: the practice of improvisation—in music and in everyday life—demands a level of attentiveness to the people with whom you are improvising and the situations in which you find yourself. Listening, as Lewis puts it, to "what the other has to play" and understanding how that playing is "related to you" entails a deep and profound sense of responsibility. As Daniel Fischlin writes in his essay on responsibility in *The Improvisation Studies Reader*, improvisation "is expressive of a codependent relation between creative iteration (call) and the response of others to that invitation to speak and sound together."[13] Over and over again, improvising artists will stress the importance of this speaking and sounding together; they will insist that learning such responsibility is a vital part of the process of acquiring attentive, empathetic, and interactive skills.

Beautiful Guidance from Some Compassionate Beings: Co-learning with Improviser-Mentors

Improvising musicians can learn a great deal by working with more experienced improvisers. Most of the improvisers we interviewed for this book talked at length about the important role that various mentors played in shaping their approach to musical improvisation. It is important to note that mentorship, in this context, is not necessarily a one-way street. Indeed, we would suggest that mentorship is best understood not in terms of a conventional pedagogy where "the teacher teaches and the students are taught," to borrow Paulo Freire's characterization of what he calls the "banking" model of education, but rather in terms of what Freire refers to as a "problem-posing education":

> Through dialogue, the teacher-of-the-students and the students-of-the-teacher cease to exist and a new term emerges: teacher-student with students-teachers. The teacher is no longer merely the one-who-teaches, but one who is himself [*sic*] taught in dialogue with the students, who in turn while being taught also teach. They become jointly responsible for a process in which all grow.[14]

Freire's point is that teachers and students are both simultaneously learners and knowledge-producers. And indeed, some of the best mentors are those who live their lives in such a way that their life becomes an embodiment of their teaching practice. Think, for instance, of saxophonist Fred Anderson. In his book on the Association for the Advancement of Creative Musicians (AACM), George Lewis tells us that Anderson had become "a hero to the younger generation, a symbol of the combination of personal tenacity, historical continuity, and radical musical integrity that many younger Chicago musicians, both within and outside the AACM, were inspired by. One reason for this respect was the Chicago community's perception that Anderson had continually sought to put into practice AACM tenets of self-reliance and independence."[15]

In an interview that was published in *Cadence* magazine in 2004, Hamid Drake describes how he received "beautiful guidance from some compassionate beings." He explicitly names Fred Anderson in this context: "When I first got into jazz," Drake explains, "one of my teachers, one of my mentors, was the great tenor saxophone player from Chicago by the name of Fred Anderson. And Fred, he was a great teacher and coach for me. He literally took me by the hand and showed me how to—of course he couldn't practice for me—but he showed me how to play this music."[16] Anderson, says Drake, "exposed me to the tradition. He guided me through this music. He taught me how to listen to it and what to listen for."[17]

The majority of the improvisers we interviewed expressed a similar level of recognition, nuance, and gratitude for the "beautiful guidance" they received from their improviser-mentors.[18] We asked: "Who are, or have been, some of your mentors? What role have they played in your development as an improvising musician?" As the range of responses is sufficiently rich, we feel it is important to quote from them at length.

GEORGE LEWIS: In terms of longevity and quality of mentorial relations, I'd say that Muhal Richard Abrams, Roscoe Mitchell, Douglas R. Ewart, Fred Anderson, Anthony Braxton, Richard Teitelbaum, David Behrman, Derek Bailey, Joel Ryan, Evan Parker, David Wessel, and Misha Mengelberg would be the most important. Rather than trying to tease out each person's specific contribution, which could end up as some sort of extended Festschrift, I could say that patience, catholicity of cultural and methodological reference, and the ability to watch someone develop without really intervening or imposing, was common to all of these people.[19]

DOUGLAS R. EWART: Joseph Jarman's work really influenced me tremendously, besides his kindness to me as a young student. His work, it was multidimensional: he was using film, he was using dance, he was using theatre, lights, poetry; and him being a writer and a musician, *and* he painted. So that impacted my work, as well as other AACM members, there was a lot of experimentation going on, so that influenced my work. . . . I bought Joseph Jarman's old alto saxophone and began to do the autodidactic approach. And then, my first lessons came from Joseph, who became a really powerful mentor for me, and one of the first people to actually not only teach me, but I played with him and he took me on tours with him. So that was how I got formally introduced to music.[20]

NORMAN ADAMS: Jeff [Reilly] started me out and continues to be a comfortable collaborator. David Mott taught me to go places I don't feel comfortable; Eddie Prévost taught me to search for new sounds and celebrate their discovery; Jerry Granelli, taught me to smile and groove; Gerry Hemingway taught me to stick with things, and not move away (for an uncomfortably long time sometimes); Joëlle Léandre taught me to leap and trust the first sound I make is a good place to start; Tim Crofts has taught me to contain my ideas and to develop them. Pauline Oliveros taught me to listen and to place myself into the sound with completely open ears, and be conscious of my listening.

All of the above were my mentors in some way. Pauline really introduced me to music that was free of rhythm and set roles, music that was organically grown from listening, not sounding. This was the great discovery. Pauline's generosity and charisma (I can't think of a better word for a person that holds whatever space she is in so gently, but so completely) was my grandmother as it were. She let me know in so many ways (verbally and non-verbally) that it was okay, that the listening will lead me in the music.[21]

ANNE BOURNE: I would say Pauline Oliveros was my most influential mentor and deepest creative relationship. I had no women teachers at university, but there was a trace of Pauline still there. When I was invited to perform with Pauline Oliveros by composer James Tenney, I had already been touring professionally for ten years with the songwriter Jane Siberry, who improvised lyrics and forms each concert as if the song was still being created. Playing a telematic improvisation with Pauline was like arriving at the destination I had been circling the world to find. With Pauline I found acceptance and deep understanding. I was never shown how to improvise, I had been given letters and words of a language of fearlessness by my early teachers of improvisation, Freddie Stone; Michael Snow, Casey Sokol, and Nobua Kubota of CCMC; Udo Kasemets, Gayle Young; John Oswald; all made a language of not knowing. And Fred Frith, knowing. Just as improvising with the live images of filmmaker Peter Mettler gave me a sense of gesture as clear as the patterns in a body of water. Pauline Oliveros with profound presence, in many moments of silence in nature, and many raucous electroacoustic sound fields we shared, showed me how to locate a universal sense of space and time, and with Ione, a recognition of being and empathy. I felt included, my voice welcomed.[22]

SUSIE IBARRA: Pauline Oliveros, Ione, Milford Graves, Nana Vasconcelos, Danongan Kalanduyan, Tania Leon, Ikue Mori, Wadada Leo Smith, Ramon Santos, Felicidad Prudente, John Zorn, and Dave Douglas have been mentors, friends, and inspirations to me in developing as a musician. They have mentored and inspired me as a performer, improviser, and composer and as a human being. I studied drum set with the late Vernel Fournier (Lester Young, Ahmad Jamal Trio), Earl Buster Smith (Sun Ra, Oscar Peterson), and Milford Graves. I studied Philippine Kulintang gong music with the late Danongan Kalanduyan.

I have learned a certain openness, freedom, concentration, and joy in listening and playing music with the late great Pauline Oliveros. I have learned how important tension is and how essential it is to create space and then jump into density when needed while also contributing to extended and nuanced textures that blend and at one point seem like one instrument in collaborative trio, Mephista with Sylvie Courvoisier and Ikue Mori. I've learned focus, the art and power of shaping and exhausting improvisation in compositions into numerous possible variations with Dave Douglas and Marc Ribot. I've learned about phrasing, breath, and lyrical rhythm with beautiful harmonies from Wadada Leo Smith. I've learned art of variation in rhythm and melody with limited notes from Danongan Kalanduyan. I've learned how much I love to create quiet ambient duets with Yuka Honda. I learned about extended technique and the wonderful discoveries in the complexities of music with the late great Derek Bailey. These are a few things that have come to my mind recently.[23]

WILLIAM PARKER: I have been lucky enough to play with many of the major figures in improvised music: Cecil Taylor, Milford Graves, Don Cherry, Grachan Monchur III, Bill Dixon, Rashied Ali, Jimmy Lyons, Frank Wright, Derek Bailey, Jeanne Lee, Matthew Shipp, Billy Higgins, Andrew Cyrille, Wilbur Ware, David S. Ware, Dave Burrell, Fred Anderson, Kidd Jordan, Hamid Drake, Daniel Carter, Billy Bang, Sunny Murray, Roy Campbell, Joe Morris, etc., etc. I have learned something from all of these musicians. The main message is: I was given the freedom to be myself, to play as fast as hard as colorful as I wanted without being penalized. I learned that all great music is a ritual about life and living and it all dances a different dance.[24]

ÉRIC NORMAND: At the beginning, Jean Derome. His music really makes me free. He is so radical and heteroclyte . . . a revelation. then meeting him and Joane [Hétu] and Martin Tétreault changed my views on music. Martin is one of kind. I was really inspired by his poetic, conceptual approach to music. . . . Then I think that my playing with Xavier Charles also recently challenged me and made me learn more and more about time . . . about space . . . at the end, my fundamentals are not musicians but writers (and also film maker JL Godard). Calvino and Perec taught me more about creation and forms than Boulez did. I'm not following a single star. I'm a heteroclyte in taste and I will hesitate if you ask if I prefer Luigi Nono to Jello Biafra. Both are important for me, as are Kagel or Japanese noise, or French songs.[25]

JARON FREEMAN-FOX: I was an apprentice of violinist Oliver Schroer from age fourteen until his death in 2008. I'd like to describe my first ever session with him: Oliver picked me up at the ferry terminal in Vancouver and drove me straight to his recording studio. He put me in the booth and came over the talkback and said "OK you're going to improvise twenty-five one-minute pieces. This first piece is called *the secret life of ants*. Start whenever you're ready."[26]

HAMID DRAKE: Certainly Don Cherry was one. And Fred Anderson played a pivotal role in my development. Pharaoh Sanders, Kidd Jordan, William Parker, Shirley Scott, Marilyn Crispell, Ken Vandermark, Kent Kessler, Yusef Lateef, David Murray, Milford Graves, and Adam Rudolph . . . the list goes on. I have been so fortunate to play with so many great artists. I continue to work with many of them. There truly are too many to name but I am grateful to them all.

I must also mention that many of my mentors have not been musicians. These are people who strengthen and inspire me in other important ways. This is integral to my deepening. They are people who wield the same spirit of improvisation through their stories and the way they live their lives. Sometimes it is only through a word or gesture or something that is written— but a seed is planted that later inspires and informs the music. It is not always linear.

The great Don Cherry (many others also) taught me how to really listen. When I was twenty-one years old, I did a short tour with him in France. Along on the tour was Trilok Gurtu, Charlie Haden, Adam Rudolph, and Doudou Gouirand. We were playing a piece that was a mixture of Don Cherry and Ornette Coleman. We had worked out how we would end the piece by utilizing a tihai. This is a phrasing played three times in succession and is often heard in Indian music. When I look back on it now, it makes me smile. I was in such a state of bliss while we were performing that I really wasn't paying attention to what was going on around me. Don recited the tihai once and then we were supposed to play it three times in succession as a group. That would end the piece. Well . . . he did that and as I said I was in such a state that I didn't know what was happening around me. Everyone stopped. Except me. It was one of those "oops moments." Back stage Don didn't scold me or say I had messed up. Nothing like that. He simply said, "Ah, I see you like the trance when you play. Trance is cool but it is also cool to be aware." That was it, but it remains as a precious teaching to this day. Awareness. Be aware of what is going on around you and within you. Listen. Listen deeply.[27]

Listening, awareness, attentiveness: these are indeed precious lessons for all musicians. The range of responses to our question about the role of improviser-mentors suggests that mentorship, in all its varied forms, is integral to the development of most improvisers. Hamid Drake's comments about nonmusical forms of mentorship ought also, perhaps, to put us in mind of our consideration of the role of autodidactism and its connection to broader social contexts: in his comments, Drake would seem to be choosing to link nonmusical elements (words, gestures, the way people live their lives) with his personal development. These connections, then, inform his playing. However, not all of the musicians with whom we spoke were uniformly enthusiastic about the idea of mentorship among improvisers. British percussionist Eddie Prévost cautions: "Be on your guard for mentors."[28] He continues:

Beware of models. Listen, learn but above all be positively critical. Look for colleagues. Be deliberative. This is the basis of a personal enlightenment that offers the possibility of serving the greater Enlightenment. I am in danger of being perceived as a mentor myself. Now approaching seventy-five years of age and continuing to convene a weekly programme of improvisation since 1999 (arising, incidentally, from my participation in a drumming clinic at Guelph [Jazz] Festival during that same year). By now, although we have never advertised our existence, way over five hundred musicians have attended from over twenty different nations. It is not, however, a teaching programme, although we all learn from each other. In this way it is collegiate and not judgmental. I only convene and keep the discipline. It is not an occasion for performance. Our workshop is a place to try out things within a collective ambiance. To try and perhaps fail. To search collectively within a sympathetic environment.[29]

Instead of mentorship as it is traditionally understood, Prévost emphasizes the importance of creating learning environments in which improvising musicians are free to experiment and take risks, learning from and with one another in a supportive, collegial atmosphere.[30] In our view, fostering and contributing to such an environment—as Prévost has done so capably—can perhaps be construed as another form of mentorship, perhaps best expressed as a form of peer-mentorship, one that embodies Freire's notion of problem-posing education and the central tenets of critical pedagogy more generally.[31] While cautioning us about conventional models of mentorship, Prévost's comments certainly highlight the importance of collaboration and community to the development of improvisational practice.

Collaboration as Classroom: Peer-to-Peer Learning in Improvised Musics

Improvisers seem to be unanimous in the view that collaboration—the experience of improvising with other musicians—is integral to the development of any improvising musician. We learn a great deal by bringing our own musical vocabularies and ideas into dialogue with those of other improvising musicians. In our experience, improvisatory encounters in which the musical sensibilities and approaches involved are substantially different from one another can provide particularly fruitful learning opportunities. Such encounters make it more difficult to rely on musical ideas that have become habitual, encouraging us instead to stretch our ears and to develop and adapt our playing to suit the new improvisatory contexts in which we find ourselves. In short, improvisers learn a great deal through the process of negotiating musical (and, by extension, social and cultural) differences in performance.

In reference to one of the central objectives for his large-scale community improvisation project called *Crepuscule*, Douglas Ewart highlights "the learning from each other, because that's the other thing about improvisation: you learn by playing with great players. You learn by playing with other improvisers, other seekers of sonic knowledge. When you come, you shine better if you're in the company of other people that are thinking too."[32]

This idea of shining better when artists are communicating in collaborative settings with like-minded improvisers is echoed by a number of musicians. When interviewed in *"Fifteen" Questions*, a music magazine that talks to some of the "leading artists of our time about their perspectives, processes and approaches," jaimie branch, the innovative American trumpeter who tragically passed away while we were in the final stages of readying this book for submission to the press, reflects on coming up in Chicago, where, in her words, "We improvise, it's not any sort of alternative, it's the way."[33] She shares a particular memory, a defining piece of improvised music she performed in 2005: "The band was two basses, two trumpets, and Evan Parker. At one point during the performance (the whole performance was less than 15 mins for sure) the other instruments faded away and left just me and Evan Parker. Those 30 seconds of duo realigned my atomic make up. Things were not the same after that. I was pushed and also pushed myself in a way that was new and so I had different expectations from then on . . . it was a good day."[34]

In an interview I (Ajay) conducted with soprano saxophonist and flautist Jane Bunnett when she took up the post of our inaugural Improviser-in-Residence in Guelph, Bunnett made a related point when asked what attracts her to improvisation: "When you're playing with like-minded musicians," she explains, "that feeling is one of the most wonderful feelings in the world. Time stops. Everything stops."[35] Bunnett, like jaimie branch, speaks about a formative moment in her experience of learning about the power of the music, a moment when, to borrow from branch, her own atomic makeup was realigned; for Bunnett, it was hearing Charles Mingus in San Francisco: "I looked at that and thought, 'This is one of the most beautiful things I've even seen. Look how the guys are communicating with each other.' And that's what really made me think I want to become . . . I want to be in, up there, in that kind of environment where everybody is communicating like that. And I was playing classical piano at the time, so when I came back from that trip it was 'finish up my piano studies, and I want to play jazz.' I knew at that point."[36]

Indeed, the idea of learning from (and learning with) the peers with whom you are performing in improvisational musical settings seems to be a vital part of the stories and the memories of many of the artists we interviewed for this book. Speaking in an interview toward the end of her weeklong role as faculty member / artist-in-residence at the Musical Improvisation at Land's End / Coin-du-Banc en folie musical improvisation camp (a community-based initiative we'll discuss in chapter five), pianist Marianne Trudel tells us that collaboration has played an "enormous" role in her development as an improvising musician. "Improvising, for me," she explains, "it's about communicating with others." Referencing the artists with whom she has had the opportunity to collaborate and how they have functioned as powerful mentors, she says, "I don't know who to name because there's so many, but there are a few encounters that really brought me a lot. Muhal Richard Abrams, when I had the privilege to work with him at the Banff Centre for the Arts, I was about twenty, I don't know, twenty-two, twenty-three maybe . . . I still feel his energy, you know, his spirit." She continues, emphasizing the ways in which these collaborators/mentors are teachers, yes, but that their way of teaching is to bring out something that's already there in the people with whom they are playing:

> And they know stuff that we don't yet. And they're so alive. They're so inspiring all these people; so Muhal, George Lewis, definitely. I had the privilege to work with them a few times, always with great joy. . . . They teach you—well they teach you yes, and no, because when you connect with these people it's . . . I was going to say they teach you to be open. . . . But it's in us already, you know? They just, they have a way to just trigger somehow, you know, something. But it's in us. I think it's in all of us.

For Trudel, "That's what's beautiful about it, because," as she explains, "let's say Muhal, you know . . . it's just this constant transfer of, I don't know, open spirit or something, you know? So there's something that just keeps being transferred and shared, and it's great. It's very powerful."[37]

Norman Adams also emphasizes the extent to which playing with other musicians has been a core part of the process of learning to improvise: "I have learned most of what I 'know' by doing," he explains, "by having the chance to play with great musicians and just trying to keep up, or letting them lead me into challenging musical situations and try to navigate myself out, or rising to the challenge of certain playing situations."[38]

When asked about the role that collaboration has played in his development as an improviser, Evan Parker stresses that "it has been fundamental. In collective improvisation at the level of making music, the ability to interact meaningfully with other players is the single most important skill." He elaborates:

> A small group of musicians based in London in the second half of the sixties including Paul Rutherford, Eddie Prévost, Trevor Watts, Derek

Bailey, Dave Holland, Kenny Wheeler, Barry Guy, and Paul Lytton gradually evolved a web of playing connections and approaches that were all connected to what is loosely called "free jazz." We were all aware to one degree or another of the need to develop original contributions. This was where I really learnt to improvise.[39]

Much like George Lewis, who tells us that "every encounter for which you foreground listening is an opportunity to transform your understanding of the situation into a mentorial one," Evan Parker states that he has learned from every musician he has listened to and with whom he has played:

By listening in the first instance to the whole "modern jazz" canon as it was available to me on records mostly, then by honing in on the work of the specific musicians I have already mentioned [Paul Desmond and John Coltrane], then working with contemporaries firstly in London and then in other European countries, I learnt from every musician I listened to and even more from the ones I played with. Again a partial list would give the wrong impression, but to have realised the ambitions of playing with Cecil Taylor, Milford Graves, Anthony Braxton, and Paul Bley gave me the privilege of coming to know them as human beings as well as musicians and in that sense they were mentors. But then so were characters closer to home like John Stevens, Derek Bailey, Alex von Schlippenbach.[40]

For an artist such as Evan Parker to suggest that he has learned from *every* musician with whom he has played (and *every* musician he has listened to) might seem an astonishing statement. But this sentiment isn't uncommon among improvising musicians. For instance, Montreal-based saxophonist Jean Derome told us, "Collaboration is central to musical improvising because, in most cases, improvising is practised in a group. Improvising is, most of the time, spontaneous collective composition. Everybody is your teacher."[41] Likewise, William Parker explained, "When you first start playing music, everybody you play with and the music itself is teaching you something. Collaboration is essential to telling the story, to writing the sound poem."[42]

Susie Ibarra similarly stresses the importance of collaboration to her own musical development: "I think collaboration is integral to my creative practice. It is something I naturally gravitate towards and I have been developing an interdisciplinary collaborative practice over the last two decades. It has informed and allowed me to grow in the way I listen, perform, and shape music as well as teaching me how to do so in solo performance as well. These are some of the ways it has expanded my improvising."[43]

Just as Ibarra views collaboration as integral to her musical development, Anne Bourne cites her first-time collaboration with drummer Susie Ibarra at the 1999 edition of the Guelph Jazz Festival as a significant encounter because of the level of "sonic empathy" that developed between them. She explains: "Listening and a willingness to attempt understanding is the way in to the landscape of an improvised piece. Directing its resonance with intention can set a tone of possibility both in the individual and in community. It can show the emergence of a way, through creative expression. I have had a beautiful experience of this communication with Susie Ibarra, among others, a sonic empathy."[44]

George Lewis also emphasizes the importance of collaboration to the process of learning to improvise:

> Collaboration has been central, because improvising with others is precisely collaboration. If you've ever played with anyone—even an interactive computer program—that is what you are doing. Without collaboration, one cannot speak of "development" as an improvisor. Or, put another way, learning to collaborate is itself an improvisative process. Beyond the stage, there can be discussions and reviews with your collaborators of what the music accomplished, which is also collaboration.[45]

Douglas Ewart's notion that "you shine better" if you perform with like-minded "seekers of knowledge"; Marianne Trudel's assertion about "something that keeps being transferred and shared" through collaboration with other improvising musicians; Norm Adams's comments about learning by rising to the challenge of collaborating with others in improvisatory musical performance; Evan Parker's insistence that he has learned from every musician he has played with and listened to; Susie Ibarra's comments that interdisciplinary collaboration has expanded her approach to improvisation; and Anne Bourne's memory of the "sonic empathy" that developed through the process of improvisatory collaboration with Susie Ibarra—these are all telling examples of how learning in improvised music takes place not only from—but, as we've been suggesting, *with*—others in a spirit of cocreative inquiry predicated on dialogue and on listening to, and learning from, others.

Stepping Forward and Stepping Back:
Jam Sessions as Contested Sites for Improvisation Pedagogy

Another model of musical co-learning, one that figures prominently in jazz cultures, is the jam session. David Ake, as we have already noted, has written about the vital role played by jam sessions as an educational process for jazz musicians. These sessions, he explains, "establish and maintain the core jazz repertoire as well as . . . performance and behavioural guidelines. . . . In short, the jam session audibly and visibly represents for beginning players what their particular jazz community expects of them, some or all of which might transfer to jazz scenes elsewhere."[46] He goes on to note that "one of the most important educational services jam sessions provide is the opportunity for beginning and intermediate musicians to play, or 'sit in,' with their more established colleagues."[47] Ake references the now legendary story (to which we alluded at the beginning of this chapter) about the Kansas City jam session in which Jo Jones humiliated Charlie Parker, prompting Parker's intense woodshedding. "Though the tale may be apocryphal," says Ake, "it clearly shows the importance of jam sessions as both a training ground and as a stage for demonstrating one's ability."[48] While these sessions are part of the lore that has surrounded the learning process for many jazz musicians, jam sessions would seem to occupy a more ambivalent place within free improvisation. Indeed, many of the improvisers we spoke with expressed discomfort with the competitive atmosphere that often characterizes jazz jam sessions and the lack of opportunities for musical experimentation therein.

In "Teaching Improvised Music," George Lewis explores the extent to which the jam session can be seen as "a social institution articulating an alternative pedagogy," and comes to the conclusion that many contemporary jam sessions "degenerate into sites for the exchange of canonized 'clichés.'"[49] In contrast to the "canonized 'clichés'" and competitiveness that often characterize the familiar model of the jazz jam session, Lewis considers the "cooperative learning" opportunities offered by two Chicago-based gatherings: the "weekly jam sessions" held at Fred Anderson's Velvet Lounge, as well as the more traditionally oriented jam sessions run by Von Freeman at the New Apartment Lounge. Lewis explains:

> Though musicians of Freeman and Anderson's generation had grown
> up under the old "cutting" regimes, the two saxophonists clearly

held no particular nostalgia for those tropes. Instead Freeman and Anderson recognized that while the "cutting session" had been of prime importance for an earlier era, the attempt to build confidence mainly through competition was not necessarily a fruitful approach for this one. Recognizing the pressures facing African-American musical creativity at that moment, cooperative learning was, for many musicians, deemed more emblematic of the music to come, especially with respect to how this music has been understood to reflect its social environment.[50]

In his interview with us for this book, Lewis expands on these comments:

I've had a rather distanced relationship to jam sessions, something I realized while reading recent ethnographic scholarship in jazz studies that documents the most recent recrudescence of the practice in New York City jazz communities. These narratives focused on the kinds of professional networks that contemporary jam sessions are fostering. These aspects of the experience could certainly be regarded as playing as much of a role in the development of a jazz improvisor as jamming itself, but what I was struck by was how little talk there was among the musicians about musical experimentation and development in the sessions.

This mode of learning through experimentation was deemed crucial to the jam session experience I grew up hearing about, but in fact I never experienced that personally in the limited experience I had with jazz jam sessions, largely around the sessions held in the early 1970s in clubs on Chicago's South Side by saxophonist Von Freeman. Von, drummer Bucky Taylor, bassist David Shipp, and pianist John Young were all very welcoming, but couldn't really be described as mentors, since they didn't really have time to talk much in the midst of what was really a performance. Rather, the sessions provided an opportunity for self-fashioning that was useful in other jazz-oriented milieus, such as the Count Basie and Gil Evans orchestras in which I participated later.

You would prepare for the sessions by studying chordal, rhythmic, and melodic materials "offline"—by yourself or with friends and colleagues. Then you could go to the jam session and call whatever tune you had been working on, secure in the knowledge that David, Bucky, Von, and "Young John Young" (as Von announced him) knew *every-*

thing. You might even get to participate in the performance of a tune you hadn't been working on.

In contrast to this, I cannot recall much in the way of jam sessions in my other life in 1970s Chicago as part of the AACM. I remember guitarist Pete Cosey organizing a session at his house once. It was supposed to become a weekly event after AACM performances, and I think Pete felt that this would help in fostering community, but it only happened once or twice.

I think that this has something to do with the extent to which jam sessions, at least in jazz, are somehow considered as "offline" with respect to a "real" performance of music. If you aren't working within or in dialogue with received models, wisdoms, and genres, what might be called jamming, perhaps, simply becomes improvising. Unlike the jazz jam sessions I experienced, which seemed relatively non-exploratory, there were already so many opportunities for exploration and experiment in the weekly performances of the AACM that I think people instinctively felt that there was no point to creating a separate "jam" experience. Maybe this realization was part of what separated what was going on in the AACM from jazz and its preoccupations with fealty to genre and tradition.

I also noticed this in my work with the first- and second-generation European free improvisors. There was never any "jamming." You just played music. Possibly this was because they had already worked out the basics of what free-improvisative interactivity meant to them before I got there around 1976. One could hear the 1975 Chicago AACM performances with the Fred Anderson Sextet as a kind of extended jamming, but only if you wanted to look at Coltrane from 1961 forward in the same way, which would seem odd to me. Of the jazz-identified experiences I had, working with Gil Evans was closest to the idea of a "jam band" like Phish or the Grateful Dead. But again, we were creating a real performance, not a flower growing in a conceptually offline hothouse.[51]

Like Lewis, many of the other improvisers we interviewed expressed ambivalence when we asked them to discuss the role that jam sessions have played in their development as improvising musicians.

NORMAN ADAMS: I don't like the term "jam sessions." It makes me
think of drum circles, or therapeutic improvisation, or improvi-

sation situations where all the music being made is "awesome" or "amazing" or "felt so good." It isn't and it doesn't! I am critical of all of my music making, whether it is improvisation, or through composed, or some combination. I look for playing situations where that critical thinking is at play. "Jam session" says, "Let's slap stuff together and see if it works" versus "Let's collaborate and make meaningful music."

Gerry Hemingway told my trio with Tim Crofts and Lukas Pearse that we need to hold some textures for longer, play louder and faster for longer, don't just stop because it starts to feel uncomfortable, keep going! Pauline [Oliveros] taught me to trust endings: when the music is finished, it's over. Marilyn Crispell brought a book of Bach sonatas for us to play. She just really wanted to play Bach, classical music, where our shared roots were! It was an honour.

The learning of improvised music has been so wonderful because it isn't about execution at all. It seems to be about pure musicality, working together, trusting instincts, knowing when to assert and when to acquiesce. Many *life* lessons![52]

ANNE BOURNE: Casey Sokol outlawed jamming in his soirees. Once you had chosen an ensemble a composition was to be improvised to its conclusion, without the continuum of people casually coming and going.

Fred Stone would tell us there should be no difference between playing and practicing. Practice as if you are in the heightened state of performance. Perform as if you are in the relaxed state of practicing. Play Free.

I tend to feel the deepest musical experiences come from improvisations that are defined by simple parameters. If there are no boundaries, or definitions a participant can be crushed by infinite possibility. A parameter can be very simple. Pauline Oliveros would say: "The way to begin? Take a deep breath, begin."[53]

JEAN DEROME: I hate jam sessions and always tried to avoid them. I never felt easy with "cutting contests" and other macho manifestations of the ego. I do enjoy playing in spontaneous musical situations and I do promote an improvisation series with chosen musicians. For example, I have been organizing the Mercredimusics improvisation series for fifteen years now in collaboration with Joane Hétu and Lori Freedman. We present twenty-four improvisation concerts a year. We follow two rules: Rule number 1 is that the combination of musicians always has to be new so that the series is not a workshop for existing or emerging groups. Our motto is: always for the first and the last time. Rule number 2 is that nothing is said prior to the improvisation.[54]

HAMID DRAKE: Jam sessions have taught me how to play, how to feel the music with others. Jam sessions taught me how to step forward and then step back. I've learned that it is not essential to play all the time. They can expose inability and vulnerability and when that happens . . . some real development takes place.[55]

JARON FREEMAN-FOX: The two examples that most stick out are times at folk festivals when a group of skilled musicians are improvising within a tradition . . . and after many hours, [the music] slowly evolves into a free improvisation, while bouncing back through the various melodies and collective musical language we have developed over the last several hours of that jam session.[56]

SUSIE IBARRA: I played a few jam sessions back in the early and mid-nineties in NYC. I played at the former Village Gate, and there was a club Visiones, and few in Harlem, and also down at the former Knitting Factory. I didn't play too many but a few. I think it was more sessions, not jam sessions, but sessions and rehearsals and performances as well as practicing on my own, that helped develop improvisation in my performance/ playing. I did play a benefit at the former Village Gate for Sun Ra where I was called up on stage to play a drum solo between Art Taylor and the Wailers and Andrew Cyrille. It was unforgettable for me. I learned about being in the moment, following through and playing your very best all at once.[57]

ÉRIC NORMAND: I'm not sure what jam means? Mostly people trying to put licks on time to make normal music, no? I prefer raw ideas to training. Most of the time, I prefer eating and talk about forms instead of jamming. Anyway the real playing is live . . . surely sometimes we play for fun.[58]

WILLIAM PARKER: I used to go to many jam sessions, some playing tunes and other jam sessions that are free. In a session you may have all kinds of musicians. The drummer begins to play a deep funk rhythm so I [used to] go with it instead of playing counterpoint. Then I learned to play funky counterpoints. The most important lesson I learned is that all music can be beautiful no matter what style. The best style for me is free.[59]

EVAN PARKER: The convention [of jam sessions] does not really exist in the same form in free improvisation performance, but there are degrees of informality in some performance contexts which allow an equivalent risk and spontaneity.[60]

EDDIE PRÉVOST: Jam sessions are rarely a place or an occasion for deliberation. And they often create a very competitive atmosphere. At best it can be a meeting of like-minded aspirants. At its worst a breeding ground for self-referentiality and possible notoriety. If this is what musicians want, then fine. It does not in my opinion present much opportunity for creative and social development. A workshop though is not a performance arena. Public presentation is a medium musicians should approach with as much conceptual deliberation as possible. Alloyed with as much joy as can be mustered! A questioning of the why am I playing rather than what am I going to play helps.

Obviously, after convening a regular workshop for over seventeen years does not mean I have no suggestions to offer my fellow travellers. I remind them all about developing skills of attentiveness and innovation—towards their instrumental material and their fellow players. These are our primary resources. And recommend within our sessions that, avoiding presentational strategies, they push themselves into situations that may not feel entirely comfortable. Remember most musicians are initially (and understandably) unsure of themselves. And, improvisers do not have the luxury of blaming a composer for the performance. With enough deliberative practice comes a confidence to freely apply the exploratory and the empathic. A negative heightened sense of self-awareness—which often reveals itself as a preoccupation with how the world perceives the subject—more than likely over-shadows memorable musical moments. I am interested in seeing the development of independent minds with perceptual powers that overcome any peacock display sequences and mature into conscious adulthood.[61]

Clearly, there is a diversity of opinion among improviser musicians when it comes to the topic of jam sessions. From dismissive remarks such as "I don't like the term jam sessions" (Norman Adams) to "I hate jam sessions and always tried to avoid them" (Jean Derome) to criticisms about the "peacock display sequences" and the "very competitive atmosphere" created though sessions that are "rarely a place or an occasion for deliberation" (Eddie Prévost), to the kind of bemused speculation expressed in comments such as "I'm not sure what jam means? mostly people trying to put licks on time to make normal music, no?" (Éric Normand), to a recognition that "the convention doesn't really exist in the same form in free improvisation performance" (Evan Parker), to admitting to "a distant relationship with jam sessions" and being critical of "how little talk there was among the musicians about musical experimentation and development in the sessions" (George Lewis)—several of the creative practitioners with whom we spoke have made it clear that the convention of jam sessions has not been central to the development of their practice as improvising musicians. Many of these musicians instead expressed a preference for "spontaneous musical situations" (Jean Derome), workshop settings (Eddie Prévost), or performance settings that allow for risk and spontaneity (Evan Parker). Others, however, remain more optimistic in their assessments, citing a range of lessons learned through jam session settings: learning that "all music can be beautiful no matter what style" (William Parker); learning "about being in the moment, following through and playing your very best all at once" (Susie Ibarra); and learning "how to play, how to feel the music with others" and "how to step forward and then step back" (Hamid Drake). Taken collectively, the ambivalence reflected in this range of responses suggests that jam sessions, despite not holding the same force, or the same currency, as they have held for jazz musicians in earlier eras, may still have some value for contemporary improvising artists, especially when, to borrow again from Lewis's remarks, they can encourage exploration and experimentation and promote "cooperative learning" instead of building competence through competition.

The emphasis on cooperative learning, so evident throughout the remarks expressed by the artists we have interviewed, prompts us to return to our discussion of the film *Whiplash* with which we began this chapter. As we return to the film, we're also put in mind of the comments we've quoted earlier from Eddie Prévost: "Be on your guard for mentors. Beware of models. Listen, learn but above all be positively critical. Look for colleagues." While the young drummer Andrew Neiman may hope to look to Fletcher as a mentor, as a co-learner, Fletcher's brutal model of dictatorial mentorship is certainly at odds with the kinds of peer-to-peer mentoring experiences and co-learning described by the musicians we've interviewed for this chapter. Far from finding a colleague in Fletcher, far from finding himself in a pedagogical environment where "we all learn from each other," Neiman is driven to succeed—if success is, in fact, what the film's dramatic finale celebrates—at a tremendous cost. There's little here to suggest anything akin to the qualities that George Lewis has identified as being common to the contribution made by some of his mentorial relations ("patience, catholicity of cultural and methodological reference, and the ability to watch someone develop without really intervening or imposing"). Little to suggest that the characters in the film are wielding the spirit of improvisation through the way they live their lives. Little to suggest that Fletcher has planted a seed that will result in positive ripple effects for a student like Nieman. Little, in fact, to suggest that Fletcher has been listening at all to "what the other has to play."

At the end of the film, the young drummer joins a band led by his vindictive bandleader on stage at a prestigious venue. But Fletcher plays one more cruel trick on Neiman with the intention of humiliating him publicly: he calls a tune that Neiman does not know and does not give him the printed score. When the tempo is counted off, Neiman falters. All of a sudden, he seems to be incapable of keeping time, let alone keeping up musically with his bandmates. In short, he cannot improvise. Perhaps he would have fared better if he had sought out the kinds of co-learning opportunities discussed in this chapter: mentorial collaborations with like-minded "seekers of knowledge" that would, as Douglas Ewart put it, enable him to shine better. Fortunately, the narrative played out in *Whiplash* bears virtually no resemblance to our own experiences of improvisation pedagogy nor to the experiences recounted by the improvising artists we've interviewed for this chapter.

 Music Festivals as Alternative
Pedagogical Institutions

In a resonant passage that puts us in mind of William Parker's comment with which we began this book, "There are many classrooms," bell hooks, in *Teaching Community: A Pedagogy of Hope*, encourages us to think of teaching and learning "as always a part of our real world experience, and our real life":

> Teachers who have a vision of democratic education assume that learning is never confined solely to an institutionalized classroom. Rather than embodying the conventional false assumption that the university setting is not the "real world" and teaching accordingly, the democratic educator breaks through the false construction of the corporate university as set apart from real life and seeks to re-envision schooling as always a part of our real world experience, and our real life. Embracing the concept of a democratic education we see teaching and learning as taking place constantly. We share the knowledge gleaned in classrooms beyond those settings thereby working to challenge the construction of certain forms of knowledge as always and only available to the elite.[1]

Like hooks, we are deeply committed to pedagogical practices that offer students and teachers innovative opportunities to reflect on the connections between academic work and broader struggles in the public arena. This is one of the reasons that we are interested in pedagogies of improvisation and improvisational pedagogies, particularly those that move beyond the walls of the classroom.

Much of our own research and teaching focuses on community-based learning as a vital model for defining and implementing educational priorities, something we will discuss in greater detail in the final chapter of this book.[2] For now, though, taking our cue from hooks, and from Cameron McCarthy and Warren Crichlow's suggestion that "an activist, interventionist slant . . . requires a much broader conception of the theatre of education than the one that currently exists in mainstream educational thinking—a notion that confines education within the walls of the classroom,"[3] we want to ask, how (and to what extent) might activist cultural practices be understood as powerful sites of pedagogical intervention? This impetus to define educational priorities in terms of such an activist orientation is, in many ways, akin to cultural critic and educator Doris Sommer's claim, in *The Work of Art in the World*, that what may begin as an artistic practice doesn't necessarily stop there. It can, as she puts it, "ripple into extra-artistic institutions and practices. Humanistic interpretation," she continues, "has an opportunity to trace those ripple effects and to speculate about the dynamics in order to encourage more movement."[4] The future of the field of critical studies in improvisation may well reside in our ability to encourage such movement, to track, analyze, and understand the impact of these ripple effects. Celebrating a growing interest in community-engaged pedagogy, and noting how students are increasingly "joining a public outside the classroom," Sommer tells us that "in the best cases, engagement combines with public scholarship to identify underrepresented creative partners who test, stretch, and refine what we learn and teach."[5]

Building on these outward-looking prompts—Parker's "many classrooms"; hooks's insistence that we attend to the ways in which teaching and learning take place both inside the classroom and out; and Sommer's call for an engaged pedagogy that can test, stretch, and refine our teaching and learning practices—we want to develop a more rigorous understanding of how alternative pedagogical institutions function in our communities, and with what impact. More specifically, we're interested in examining the roles that arts presenters—festival organizers, curators, venue owners—play as community-based educators and activists.

For one thing, arts presenters play an important role in providing opportunities for improvising musicians to hear, see, and learn from other improvisers. As we note in chapter one, audio and video recordings can be very helpful educational resources, but some lessons are best learned through the experience of live musical performances. Recall, for example, our discussion of Gerry Hemingway's eye and ear-opening performance at the 1996 edition of the Guelph Jazz Festival. In addition to providing important opportunities for improvising musicians to share musical knowledge with one another (particular musical techniques, for example), music festivals and venues play a vital role as cultural gate-keepers more broadly, exposing musicians and the wider public to new musical ideas. For example, as a teenager in the early 1990s, I (Jesse) spent many evenings at various jazz clubs in Toronto, trying to learn as much as I could about jazz drumming. In retrospect, one venue played a particularly important role in my musical education, a club known as the Bermuda Onion, which has long since closed. In addition to hearing—and meeting—many of my musical heroes that I knew from recordings (including Elvin Jones, Max Roach, and Tony Williams), I was exposed to many musicians and musical ideas that were new to me. Two Bermuda Onion performances that stand out for me in this regard were the Oliver Lake Quartet in 1990 and the Sun Ra Arkestra in 1991. I had no prior knowledge of Lake's or Ra's music. I had not really heard of "free jazz" or "free improvisation." But I had come to trust the programming at the Bermuda Onion, so I attended both performances, which were reve-latory to me, broadening my musical worldview and my conception of jazz, exposing me to models of musical improvisation and drumming that I did not know existed. Those performances, like all musical performances, took place within a particular institutional context that served an important pedagogical function in my musical development.

Arts organizations, including music venues, festivals, and concert series, also have an important role to play in shaping our understanding of, and engagement with, the wider public sphere. As the founding artis-tic director of the Guelph Jazz Festival from 1994 to 2016, an arts orga-nization dedicated to presenting innovative jazz and creative improvised music, I (Ajay) am aware of the ways in which the choices I make (about what artists to present, in what context, etc.) ought to be understood not simply as programming matters, but as complex and resonant pedagogi-cal acts, acts that frequently question static relations of power, acts that seek to build alternative visions of community and social cooperation, acts that often explicitly set out to challenge taken-for-granted represen-tations and assumptions. Programming decisions, in other words, are far from neutral: they involve choices that are connected in complex and important ways to broader struggles over resources, identity formation, and power. Festivals can provide meaningful opportunities to recast the histories, identities, and epistemologies of diverse (and often marginal-ized) peoples, to stage diversity, and to promote counternarratives that invite and enable an enlargement of the base of valued knowledges. In this context, festivals might purposefully be considered, in writer, cultural commentator, and arts policy consultant Max Wyman's terms, as "testing grounds for new visions of how we live together, new ways to establish shared values."[6] Moreover, as sociologist Jonathan Wynn argues in his book *Music/City*, festivals are rarely examined sites of place making, sites "that can tell us something about how fleeting moments can set in motion a great many actors and assets for longer-term impact."[7]

In short, the potential of arts presentation to shape musical currents and, indeed, to define communities shouldn't be underestimated. Keeping in mind Kalle Lasn's notion of culture jamming, we want to suggest that festivals, as alternative pedagogical institutions, can offer vital sites for jamming the classroom. Festival organizers are particularly well positioned to prompt what Lasn calls "perspective-jarring turnabouts," not only by unsettling categorically sanctioned ways of seeing, thinking, and listening, but also by intervening in our understanding of issues as important as history, community, culture, taste, and value. Jamming the classroom, in other words, necessarily entails a shifting set of roles and responsibilities for cultural gatekeepers and teachers.

In their book *Free Spaces: The Sources of Democratic Change in America*, Sara Evans and Harry Boyte ask, "Where are the places in our culture through which people sustain bonds and history? What are the processes through which they may broaden their sense of the possible, make alliances with others, develop the practical skills and knowledge to maintain democratic organization?"[8] We believe that there's something about the presentation of improvised musics in particular that enables the kind of pedagogical and cultural work that Evans and Boyte identify. We'd like to use this chapter to open up questions about the extent to which the presentation of improvised musics might offer opportunities for aggrieved communities to assert their own rights while educating the public on matters of social justice and advancing the struggle for more inclusive frameworks of understanding.

Throughout the history of jazz and creative improvised music, as we've argued elsewhere, creative practitioners have worked as catalysts for collective social action and community development.[9] Think, for example, of the work of Horace Tapscott and the Union of God's Musicians and Artists Ascension in Los Angeles, or the projects associated with the Association for the Advancement of Creative Musicians in Chicago. Indeed, many artists have made a direct difference in their communities by working together to voice new forms of social organization, to "sound off" against oppressive orders of knowledge production, to create opportunities and develop resources for disadvantaged people. In doing so, they've played a powerful role in recasting the identities and histories of aggrieved populations and in promoting self-representational counternarratives to dominant understandings of music and culture. Arts presenters have an important role to play not only in supporting such musics and musicians, but also in bringing their message to the attention of a wider public, thereby expanding the base of knowledges to which people have access and value.

In making such claims, we've taken our prompt from George Lipsitz's compelling argument that "those of us who work, teach, and study as 'traditional intellectuals' in institutions of higher learning have an important role to play in analyzing and interpreting the changes that are taking place around us. We need to develop forms of academic criticism capable of comprehending the theorizing being done at the grassroots level by artists and their audiences, of building bridges between different kinds of theory."[10] The kind of grassroots, community-based theorizing Lipsitz refers to is played out not just through the work of artists and their audiences, but also through the activity of arts organizations and institutions. Clearly, this isn't necessarily a comfortable theory for all (or perhaps even for most) arts organizations. For many large-scale, corporate-run festivals, the notion that arts presentation should in any way be likened to activist pedagogical practices might seem a far stretch. Tourism geographer Bernadette Quinn claims that "the proliferation of festivals is at least partially explained by a formulaic approach to duplicating festivals found to have been 'successful' in particular city contexts."[11] In her analysis of the rise and popularity of urban arts festivals, Quinn suggests that there is a growing tendency to neglect the social value of festivals in favor of an emphasis on economic outcomes. We understand (all too well) the financial risks and challenges of running a music festival and/or concert series. Nevertheless, what interests us is how a growing number of arts organizations specializing in improvised music might be understood in the context of an argument about arts presentation as a form of activist critical pedagogy.[12] In addition to the Guelph Jazz Festival, annual celebrations of improvised music, including the Vision Festival in New York City, Le festival international de musique actuelle in Victoriaville, and the Suoni Per Il Popolo festival in Montreal, each play an important pedagogical role in their respective communities.

George Lewis—whose own stewardship of improvisative musicality has done much to generate fresh new understandings and perspectives of improvisation—has made similar arguments about saxophonist Fred Anderson. Lewis cites Anderson's club, the Velvet Lounge, as an alternative pedagogical institution,[13] noting how the venue has directly nurtured improvisational music-making initiatives by providing a place for musicians to play on Chicago's South Side. Lewis is right to point to the vital role that such alternative pedagogical institutions can play in our communities. But rather than examine how such pedagogical institutions can inform improvisative practice (or even pedagogical practice more broadly), we're interested in trying to develop a different understanding of how the alternative institutions affiliated with improvisatory practice serve as testing grounds for broader visions of community and soundings of social cooperation that might enable us to edge toward a more just world.

This line of inquiry, we understand, runs the risk of being interpreted as a kind of glorified advertisement for the festivals and arts organizations with which we have been involved. This is not our intention; rather, we want to share some of our own experiences as presenters and producers (as well as performers and audience members at performances) of improvised music in the hope that they might be instructive to other cultural workers and educators, and to students of improvisation whom we hope will seek out opportunities to experience live performances of improvised music. We acknowledge that there are limits to our argument about arts presentation as a form of critical practice. Just as not all acts of musical improvisation are successful, not all improvised music is anti-hegemonic. Indeed, there are many instances of improvisation that do not work in the model ways we are suggesting, and these instances need to be confronted squarely and honestly. For example, many of the spaces associated with improvised music and improvised music education continue to be largely male-dominated, perpetuating the masculinist ethos that has surrounded many aspects of jazz culture and improvised music historically. In our view, the varied sites associated with improvisation pedagogy—including festivals and venues that feature improvised music—have an important role to play in challenging and dismantling hegemonic assumptions about gender.

At this point, we want to acknowledge a possible tension between our roles as arts presenters/educators and the implications that such roles might have for our expectations of musicians. Clearly, there is a huge difference between, on the one hand, noting the activism of particular musicians and, on the other, implying that musicians, because of the music's potential to affect the social sphere, ought to be held morally responsible for that power. This is tricky territory. Throughout the long and complex history of debate on this issue, musicians have rightly been critical of the ways in which their lifework has too often been reduced (by academics, journalists, industry executives, marketers, etc.) to suit particular frameworks of assumption.[14] The very act of articulating some of the principles and patterns that guide our practice as arts presenters runs the risk of being interpreted as an imposition of our own political agenda on the artists we present. We do tend to program particular artists whose work is akin to our own tastes, values, commitments, and pedagogical priorities. And, of course, these choices take place within the context of (and are often complicated by) financial, institutional, and material constraints.

Our point here is not that we must, as arts presenters/educators, find ways to insist that the musicians we program explicitly adhere to particular moral or pedagogical principles; rather, we want to consider the extent to which the act of presentation itself can itself be understood as a form of pedagogical activism. As presenters, our programming choices and omissions inevitably reflect some kind of interest, whether it be racial, gendered, national, or something other. While it's impossible to predict the outcome of our work as arts presenters/educators, it is our belief that the community-based pedagogical work of arts organizations has the potential to challenge dominant habits of response, judgment, and understanding.

In his book *The Defiant Imagination: Why Culture Matters*, Max Wyman makes a convincing case for the pedagogical value of arts and culture, suggesting that "engagement with artistic creativity develops the ability to think creatively in ways that significantly enlarge the educational experience. It encourages the flexible, nuanced thinking that will be an essential requirement of any innovative response to the challenges we face. It makes us see our world in fresh ways, encourages suppleness of mind. Doubt is cast on our most comfortable perceptions. We learn the art of adaptability."[15] In our work as presenters, performers, and scholars of improvised music, we have tended to focus on modes of music making that we feel are in keeping with Wyman's argument: musics that foreground issues of community and freedom of expression, encouraging flexible, nuanced, and adaptive thinking. Although Wyman does not write specifically about improvisation, many of his assertions—about art's ability to foster an openness to different points of view, its insistence on educating us for uncertainty, its capacity "to change attitudes, to foster the mutual respect that will help ensure a more peaceful world"[16]—are akin to the claims we've made elsewhere about the capacity of impro-vised musics to foster social mobility for members of subordinated social groups, and to trouble the assumptions fostered by dominant systems of representation.[17] As presenters of improvised music, our work is largely about providing alternatives to the taken-for-granted course of things, about creating new knowledges and opportunities, about generating alternative ways of seeing and hearing the world.

Improvisation, in short, can play a signally important role in cultivat-ing resources for hope. It speaks directly to the risks we need to take in order to create opportunities for change, in order to envision a more hopeful, more just world in the face of the degradations and injustices that beset us. As Wyman notes, "It is the artist who helps us hope, helps us learn that . . . better possibilities exist."[18] With this in mind, we think that it behooves us, as arts presenters, to create opportunities for such hope and learning. In the spirit of advancing such a goal, we return to the work of bassist and multi-instrumentalist William Parker, whose practice of improvisational music making is largely predicated on the need for hope. "In order to survive," Parker tells us, "we must keep hope alive,"[19] reminding us that hope is a necessity in face of the degradations that beset aggrieved populations around the globe.

Parker, in addition to being a musician, is also an arts organizer. Along with his partner, Patricia Nicholson, Parker is one of the driving forces behind New York's artist-run Vision Festival, a festival of "Free Jazz Arts" that explicitly articulates its own mandate in the context of broader struggles for social awareness. The theme of the 2004 edition of the festival, "Vision for a Just World," made clear the organizers' com-mitments: "It is imperative," the festival announced on its home page, "that we respond to the erosion of rights in America and the new and very dangerous Imperialism abroad."[20] In an effort to resist the "deaden-ing effects of fear, conformity and greed," the Vision Festival—which, from its inception has been "committed to combining social awareness and presenting the very best visionary music and art"—seeks to provide a platform for community response and involvement. Included as part of the program that year was a panel discussion, "The Artist's Role in Waging Peace," where artists featured at the festival talked about their art in the context of urgent issues of social responsibility. Worth noting again is the way in which a community-based arts organization explicitly frames its programming mandate as a kind of activist pedagogy for hope. And it's no coincidence that Vision Festival organizers have, in their own words, heeded "the democratic model implicit in jazz improvisation, in which a group of individuals rises together as a collective voice." With the help of such a model, the organizers proclaim, we will "build a bridge to the future."[21]

Vision Festival's parent organization, Arts for Art, continues to educate for social change through the Vision Festival and a range of other arts initiatives. Since 2011, for example, Arts for Art has offered the Visionary Youth Orchestra, a cost-free weekly after-school program for young people aged eleven to eighteen who are given an opportunity to "study the repertoire of the giants of Free Jazz and learn to improvise freely."[22] In January 2017, Arts for Art founded a group called Artists for a Free World, which "takes a stand for racial & economic justice to create a world where peace is possible."[23] Artists for a Free World explicitly supports human rights including nondiscrimination and immigration rights, environmental issues, and free speech, as well as issues affecting artists such as government support for the arts, and copyright law reform. In just two years, Artists for a Free World have participated in over forty political demonstrations, using the power of musical improvisation to sound off against oppression and cultivate resources for hope.

When we asked William Parker about the links among arts presentation, education, and hope, he suggested that arts presentation could be understood as "a doorway to enter into the realm of hope."[24] Specifically, he talked about how the work of arts organizations helps in vital ways to "keep the world afloat" and about how the world would be significantly diminished without festivals of improvised music. "The world is eroding," Parker explained, "and music helps to stop the erosion."[25] Parker's comments take on added urgency in light of the actions of former American president Donald Trump, a man who actively denies climate change, who has openly mocked persons with disabilities, and has bragged about his history of sexually assaulting women. At a time when increased xenophobia threatens to impoverish our collective futures, hope may well reside in people's capacity to ask fresh questions, think critically, and not take what they see and hear for granted. This is no small matter in an era when positions are becoming more and more entrenched and polarized, when forms of public expression are increasingly being co-opted by corporate priorities that are becoming naturalized and accepted as self-evident, and when the very possibilities for dissonant frameworks of understanding have been enfeebled. If, as philosopher Mary Zournazi suggests in her book *Hope: New Philosophies for Change*, hope is "the force which keeps us moving and changing . . . so that the future may be about how we come to live and hope in the present,"[26] then we have much to learn from arts organizations, like the Vision Festival, that strive to find ways to build bridges to the future, that strive to articulate resources for hope in their insistence that a better world is possible. Such an insistence necessitates fresh pedagogical approaches to arts programming, including the presentation of improvisation, which emboldens us to take risks and to recognize, as bell hooks rightly reminds us, that "the willingness to change and be changed, to remain always open is a defining principle of intellectual [and we would add creative] life."[27]

If, with hooks, we accept the notion that the community needs to be understood as a vital site for pedagogical practice, and we seek to "re-envision schooling as always a part of our real world experience," then it's important for us to reflect on the complexity of networks through which improvised music happens. How do institutional frameworks shape not only what we listen to as well as how and where we listen, but also the very ways in which we negotiate and construct meaning? Who has the institutional power to determine what "counts" as knowledge, as history, as music (or as noise), and in what ways is that power connected to broader structures of social control? To what extent has our reception (and perhaps even our assessment) of improvised music been determined by dominant epistemic and educational frameworks, by elite networks of power and privilege? How can cultural institutions shape assumptions about public value, social inclusion, and cultural legitimacy? How do festivals and arts organizations that present, market, and promote adventurous and avant-garde forms of music make pedagogical interventions in the very fields of critical understanding that surround them by supporting the expression of musical ideas that are not widely known or supported?

In asking such questions, we are indebted to the Freirian principle of demythologizing: the need to put critical pressure on the assumptions, languages, histories, and narratives promulgated by dominant discourses and pedagogies. The programming decisions that I (Jesse) made in my capacity as the artistic director from 2005 to 2008 of NUMUS—a presenter and producer of "new music" based in Waterloo, Canada—sought, for example, to challenge received ideas concerning what constitutes "new music," a term that has served a decidedly narrow set of class, race, and gender interests historically as evidenced by the whitewashed programming of many new music festivals, and by most academic and journalistic discussions of new music, which have focused disproportionately on music composed by white men. By programming musics and musicians representing a wide variety of cultural, social, gender, and musical contexts—including numerous performances of improvised musics—I critically examined my own assumptions about new music and, I hope, encouraged audience members and other arts presenters to do likewise. In and of itself, this shift in musical programming was hardly revolutionary. However, the expanded curatorial focus has continued in the more than ten years since I left the organization. Now under the artistic direction of improvising clarinetist Kathryn Ladano, NUMUS has continued to present and produce concerts of experimental music that represent a broad range of cultural and musical communities, including many improvisatory ones.

In addition to offering such critical prompts, arts presenters can provide a testing ground for alternative ways of being in the world. As David Picard and Mike Robinson argue in their book *Festivals, Tourism and Social Change: Remaking Worlds*, festivals "generate symbolic adaptations and alternatives to existing states" and "initiate change that could modify existing states."[28] Picard and Robinson go on to argue that "the festival needs to be linked to the wider sociological, economic and political context of change, as a site to adapt, reconstruct and re-enact meaningful narrations of the collective being in the—globally enlarged—world."[29] They continue, "Festivals draw our attention as participants, tourists and scholars precisely because they provide moments of time and space to reflect upon our being in the world and questions of collective meaning and belonging."[30]

New visions of how we might live together. Time and space to reflect upon questions of collective meaning and belonging. Actors and assets for long-term impact. Staging and narrating collective being in the—globally enlarged—world. These are large claims, and they constitute rather a tall order for festivals to fulfill. But we've put such claims on the table here because they offer a compelling commentary on the role that festivals can play in activating diverse energies of critique and inspiration, and of the difference they can make—and have made—in their communities by creating time and space to sound, and to stage, new forms of social organization.

In his book *Genuine Multiculturalism: The Tragedy and Comedy of Diversity*, sociologist and novelist Cecil Foster tells us that "life is messy: it is about different and diverse people having no bigger challenge than to get along together . . . an achievement for which there is no guarantee."[31] Cultural theorist Ien Ang has made a similar suggestion: "One of the most urgent predicaments of our time," she writes, "can be described in deceptively simple terms: how are we to live together in this new century?"[32] This question takes on particular urgency in light of the mass migration of people across the globe because of persecution and war in their homeland, and the widespread failure of state policies to protect individual rights. In his book *Racism and Cultural Studies: Critiques of Multiculturalist Ideology and the Politics of Difference*, E. San Juan Jr. suggests that "the most serious problems involving racism, ethnic conflicts, nationality disputes, economic deprivation, environmental damage, migrant workers, trade in women's bodies, drugs, and so on . . . seem to multiply and accumulate, demanding interpretation and new methods of elucidation."[33] In such contexts, we want to suggest, the staging and sounding of diversity that festivals can enable may have a valuable, if unsuspected, role to play in showing different ways of negotiating difference and advancing the struggle for a more inclusive repertoire of valued knowledges.

When improvising musicians come together across boundaries of difference, as they often do during performances at festivals, venues, and concert series such as those we've mentioned in this chapter, they provide a modest, but perhaps also a profound, response to the predicament Ang identifies: they engage with one another in a meaningful way to cocreate something new. One of the core lessons of improvised music is that it can teach us to work together to enact the possibilities that we collaboratively envision. George Lipsitz has put it this way: "What critics and curators often describe as community-based art making is better described as art-based community making—a form of democratic interaction that enacts the just social relations that social movements often only envision."[34]

While it may be tempting to think about music festivals as sites that remove us from the everyday, that create places and spaces that are somehow separate from our daily lives, we would argue that our experiences at festivals and other public events are very much "a part of our real world experience, and our real life," to return again to the bell hooks quotation with which we began this chapter. Indeed, music festivals can be fruitfully thought of as an example of what sociolegal scholar Davina Cooper has described as "everyday utopias." Everyday utopias, Cooper writes, "don't place their energy on pressuring mainstream institutions to change, on winning votes, or on taking over dominant social structures. Rather they work by creating the change they wish to encounter."[35] The changes that we, and many like-minded activist/educators, would like to see include greater recognition of, and dialogue among, diverse voices in society, particularly those of marginalized communities. Performances of improvised music are well suited to enact such changes and to function as "everyday utopias": musicians from diverse backgrounds who may not have even met each other prior to the performance are able to come together, listen to one another, and engage in meaningful dialogue across various forms of difference. And, importantly, what may have begun as artistic practice, to return to Doris Sommer's claim in *The Work of Art in the World*, doesn't necessarily stop there: it can, as Sommer suggests, "ripple into extra-artistic institutions and practices." Efforts to build the curatorial capacities of performing arts organizations in ways that promote a broadening and a diversifying of the base of valued knowledges can encourage such ripple effects. In doing so, such efforts have a vital role to play in enabling generative new forms of community-making, critical thinking, and social practice. In his book on music festivals, Jonathan Wynn makes a related point when he suggests that "understanding how festivals fit into a city's overall cultural landscape means knowing what happens not only during the festival, but after it as well."[36] He notes that "impact reports mostly highlight monetary gains," but that they often "fail to encompass each longer term change to cities at the ground level, as everyday folks experience them."[37] While "numbers of visitors, and especially numbers of visitor dollars, are persuasive measures," he writes, these kinds of statistics tend to "miss the lived processes, interactions, experiences, and perspectives"[38] that need to be seen as a vital part of the long-term impact, the broader ripple effects, associated with music festivals.

As we make the case that festivals might be purposefully understood as activist sites and alternative pedagogical institutions, as we seek to understand these "broader ripple effects," we are inclined to ask how we ought to evaluate a festival's success or impact. Rather than relying on the conventional indicators such as "bums in seats" or a festival's profit margin, what if we asked how many lives have been changed by the music we present at our festivals, and in what ways?

Life-changing experience: this is a phrase we hear regularly about the work associated with (and performed by) the arts organizations with which we have been involved. And we hear it from musicians, from audience members, even from critics. We mention this not to tout our own accomplishments. Rather, we're interested in trying to understand the "perspective-jarring turnabouts" (to quote again from Kalle Lasn) that might be enabled through the presentation of improvised music. What is it, in other words, about improvised music that prompts such responses?[39]

It may well be that the singularity of improvised musical performance, the fact that the music exists only in the moment in which performers and audience alike experience it as a shared experience, allows the music to reach so deeply into our consciousness that we feel changed by the experience. But we want to suggest that it's not just the music that prompts such a turnabout. More suggestively, perhaps, it's a question of how improvised music is (or isn't) taken up in our culture. The experience of improvised music is fundamentally shaped by the institutions and practices through which the music is presented, discussed, talked about, taught, marketed, reviewed, circulated, and listened to. As we've been arguing throughout this book, these are important matters that are connected to issues of resources, power, identity formation, and public interest.[40] We want to hold onto the belief that the agency demonstrated in the work of small independent or artist-run festivals (often battling corporate-dominated interests) should not be underestimated. Sure, we need to keep in mind the role that schools, magazines, funding agencies, record labels, award ceremonies, government organizations, and other institutions play in mediating the flow of improvised music. And yes, the presentation of improvised music in a festival setting certainly involves its fair share of compromises and accommodations; we wouldn't want to underestimate the significant role that material constraints and conditions play in shaping the music. The everyday realities of fundraising, marketing, ticket revenues, and production costs, among others, will always be there as contexts and constraints to be taken into consideration when programming a festival. Of course we'd be remiss, as arts presenters, not to take them into account, just as we would be remiss not to acknowledge that improvised musical encounters don't *always* function in the liberatory ways we might be envisioning.[41] But let's also hold onto the transformative potential of culture in general, and music in particular. As the authors of *Legible Practices*—a book about social innovation and the "rewiring of institutions" written under the auspices of the Helsinki Design Lab—have suggested, "Culture is the ultimate engine of scale for any innovation in society. Without changing cultural values and meanings it is difficult if not impossible for new social relationships to propagate or for new approaches to flourish."[42]

Our argument here is that this kind of large-scale change in cultural values (which, we believe, can happen when we "jam the classroom") necessarily takes place within a multidimensional field of understanding. The presentation of improvised music in a festival setting may not, in and of itself, necessarily create such change; however, once we begin to theorize and practice arts presentation within the context of broader social change discourses and movements, as has happened explicitly with a number of the arts presenters we've discussed in this chapter, the transformative potential of our work takes on new shape. Lewis suggests that it's important for us, as educators, to challenge what has become a set of common refrains among music students: Why do we need to talk about the music? Can't we just play?[43] Putting critical pressure on such notions, as well as on the assumption that "hearing music is more important than reading about it" is,[44] we think, a crucial step in the kind of field-building and community-building that may ultimately enable the activist pedagogical interventions that interest us.

In an effort to bring together my community interests and involvement with my academic work, I (Ajay) organized a conference at the University of Guelph in 1996 as part of the Guelph Jazz Festival's regular schedule of events. Since that time, the Guelph Jazz Festival Colloquium has become an annual international conference that has been bringing together scholars, creative practitioners, and audiences for vibrant and inspired critical exchanges for over two decades. The work associated with the colloquium (talks and panel discussions, published papers, and, perhaps most importantly, the creation of a highly integrated and diverse network of international scholars) has done much to build an audience for the music that is heard during the festival.

The Guelph Jazz Festival Colloquium also has led to the formation of two large-scale partnership-based research initiatives: Improvisation, Community, and Social Practice (ICASP) and the International Institute for Critical Studies in Improvisation (IICSI). As we will discuss in chapter four, both research initiatives have played a key role in shaping critical studies in improvisation as a new field of academic inquiry. Using our experiences in Guelph as a model for partnerships between music festivals and universities, members of the ICASP and IICSI teams are now organizing satellite conferences in Montreal, Vancouver, St. John's, and Regina in Canada, as well as conferences in Athens and Paris. In addition to holding at least three conferences a year, we have a book series, a peer-reviewed academic journal (*Critical Studies in Improvisation / Études critiques en improvisation*), and numerous graduate students and postdoctoral fellows getting jobs in a variety of scholarly fields, including improvisation studies. The field-building and the community-building we're describing have set something in motion that I (Ajay) certainly couldn't have predicted when I started a jazz festival in Guelph many years ago. But herein lies a tale of sustainability—of capacity unleashed through cross-sectoral and multidimensional forms of collaboration. To the extent that Guelph now plays host to a festival that is internationally lauded as an agent of cultural change,[45] it's important to recognize that the Guelph Jazz Festival is more than just a festival. It's part of a broader pedagogical field of social and cultural understanding in which experimental and improvised practices are at the core.

As we've already noted, music, in and of itself, cannot be a simple corrective for all of the world's problems. But if the exercise of human rights becomes meaningful not only through the existence of covenants and treaties, but also as a result of the broader cultures of consciousness and obligation that help transform those rules into acknowledgment and action, then we would suggest that a radical reorganization of our priorities seems very much to be in order. And this applies not only to policymakers and to political agenda setters, but also to all of us—artists, educators, citizens—working for a better world.

As presenters working with improvising musicians, we have a role to play in cultivating purposeful resources for listening, to provide our audiences with encounters that encourage them to hear the world anew. Improvised music accentuates the dialogic nature of performance and grants agency to (and places responsibility on) listeners to find their own pathways through the work. Also at issue is the need to create more equitable and non-market-driven structures of inclusion. Taking such a challenge seriously means attending rigorously to matters of diversity (of race, gender, and sexuality, etc.), not only in terms of the artists we present, but also at the level of our audience members, our boards of directors, our staff, and even our sponsors. In short, we need to think of the presentation of improvised music as an opportunity to animate and to transform public understanding. We believe that arts organizations dealing with improvised music-making offer a particularly resonant space in our culture for precisely this kind of work.

We are not alone in thinking this way. Among the many people we continue to encounter (and interact with) through our various roles, many clearly see it as a priority for musicians, presenters, and listeners alike to build inclusive activist communities of concern and commitment. None pretend to have easy solutions. But many offer their work as a model for new forms of social mobilization, more just ways of understanding, and new kinds of activist pedagogy. All, in their own ways, are insistent in sounding their belief that another world *is* possible. All, in their own ways, exemplify hooks's notion that teaching and learning are going on constantly. And herein, we believe, lies a message of hope. In our own modest ways, this is the message we'd like people to hear in so much of the music we present, as well as in the events, discussions, and educational endeavors that take place around our festivals.

FOUR | Improv Goes to School

Musical Improvisation and the Academy

In his 1983 essay, "Improvisation: Towards a Whole Musician in a Fragmented Society," improvising violinist Malcolm Goldstein asks,

> How is it that we have so thoroughly omitted improvisation from the experience / musicianship / training of students in practically every college and music conservatory? . . . or perhaps it would be more accurate to say "excluded?!" And, if it has been excluded, then what does such an act tell us about our culture, attitudes, and value systems? What we choose to teach, what we choose to enact and share informs us as to what we consider valuable, to be perpetuated and socially acknowledged.[1]

The things we choose to teach—or, as Goldstein points out, not to teach—have a vital impact on the value that educational institutions, and society more generally, place on different forms of knowledge production and, indeed, on what "counts" as knowledge.

Concerns similar to those voiced by Goldstein are echoed in much of the literature on the pedagogy of musical improvisation. Writing in *Music Educators Journal* in 1996, for example, Paul Goldstaub argues that "the time has come for every institution that trains music teachers to take an active role in developing programs that promote and teach improvisation. Sadly, very few schools are doing this."[2] In their book *Free to Be Musical: Group Improvisation in Music*, Patricia Shehan Campbell and Lee Higgins put it this way: "We have observed many more words than actual practices in the placement of improvisation within the process of a truly musical education."[3]

While improvisation has yet to take hold within music education as fully as these and other writers (including us) would like, there have been numerous positive developments in recent years, developments that are having a far-reaching and paradigm-shifting impact within academic institutions. For example, in 2016 the College Music Society published a document titled "Transforming Music Study from Its Foundations: A Manifesto for Progressive Change in the Undergraduate Preparation of Music Majors" by Patricia Shehan Campbell, David Meyers, and Ed Sarath. This important publication advocates for a reorientation of undergraduate music curricula in order to equip students with the "foundational skills that a musician in the twenty-first century will need. These skills include the ability to improvise; to compose music relevant to the times; to perform well; to teach effectively; and to think critically about the role of music, realizing all of its contemporary and historical diversity."[4] In addition to interpretive performance (which remains the primary focus for most university music majors), the document calls for undergraduate music programs to broaden their focus to include improvisation and composition, thereby training a new generation of "improviser-composer-performers."

Academic interest in musical improvisation is further evidenced by the growing number of improvisers to have received academic appointments at major universities. A partial list includes the following: Wadada Leo Smith, Vinny Golia, and the late Charlie Haden at the California Institute for the Arts; Anthony Braxton at Wesleyan University; Roscoe Mitchell and Fred Frith, both previously at Mills College; George Lewis at Columbia University; Anthony Davis and Mark Dresser at the University of California, San Diego; Myra Melford at the University of California, Berkeley; the late Milford Graves and the late Bill Dixon at Bennington College; Casey Sokol at York University; Nicole Mitchell at the University of Pittsburgh; Vijay Iyer at Harvard University; and the late Pauline Oliveros at Rensselaer Polytechnic Institute. "Such academic positions," as David Ake has noted in his essay "Learning Jazz, Teaching Jazz," "appear particularly attractive to musicians in light of the medical and retirement benefits available through school employment, especially given the uncertain future that hung over so many jazz performance venues and record labels at the turn of the twenty-first century."[5] For Ake, these musicians/teachers counter "the adage that 'those who can, do; others teach,' as jazz musicians—young and old—increasingly consider the college classroom, rather than neighbourhood sessions, to be the prime training ground for beginners."[6]

The increasing number of improvising artists now working and teaching within the academy might help to redress a concern articulated by Ingrid Monson in her book *Saying Something*. Monson's book, in part, is an effort to respond to "a long-standing grievance in the jazz community: previous writers had not taken the perspectives and interpretations of jazz musicians seriously in their works."[7] We would argue that there is an analogous argument to be made about how the perspectives of improvising artists have been elided (or unacknowledged) in dominant histories and narratives of the music. Will this change, we wonder, as more improvising musicians enter into the academy as teachers, as producers, as mobilizers of knowledge? We certainly share Monson's concern with "the place of human agency, lived experience, and vernacular knowledge in the interpretive acts of academia,"[8] and believe that academic work can only be enriched by the insider perspectives of improvising artists.

In this chapter, we examine the changing historical relationships between musical improvisation and the academy, as well as some of the implications of those relationships for both the academy and the field of musical improvisation itself. We focus primarily on the relationships between improvisation and the academy in North America, where the majority of our professional experience has taken place. First, we will provide a brief discussion of the history of improvisation in Western art music, a history that has shaped—and continues to shape—music pedagogy within the academy.

It is well documented that there were numerous improvisatory musical traditions in Western musical discourse prior to the twentieth century. Many of the great classical, baroque, and Romantic composers, including Bach, Haydn, Mozart, and Liszt, were accomplished improvisers—a practice that was often a crucial aspect of their approach to the compositions for which they have come to be better known. Improvisation took place in the ornamentation of notated parts, in solo preludes and cadenzas, in fugal church organ playing, and more.[9] With the exception of improvised church organ music, most other improvisatory traditions within Western art music had greatly diminished, if not disappeared entirely, by the middle to late nineteenth century. There are several reasons for this disappearance, notably changes in the political economy surrounding music precipitated by the dominance of printed sheet music.[10]

By the nineteenth century, sheet music had firmly established itself as the primary medium for the dissemination of music. This effectively turned music into a commodity that could be copyrighted and mass-produced, exposing composers' music to a much wider market and allowing for a potentially far greater monetary return. It seems quite likely that the eventual dominance of the printed score contributed to the near disappearance of improvised modes of music making in the Western classical tradition. Improvised musical performances simply weren't as marketable or profitable as printed music.[11]

With the decline of improvisation in Western art music traditions came corresponding shifts in the discourses surrounding those traditions; improvisation came increasingly to be thought of as "the other" of musical composition, not only as a musical process, but also in terms of its social status. This "othering" of improvisation is implicit in some of the earliest dictionary usages of the word "improvisation" (and variations thereof). For example, the 1795 edition of the Oxford English Dictionary states: "The Italian improvisator never attempts a ballad without striking his mandolino." The 1811 edition of the OED associates improvisation with "the flexibility of Italian and Spanish languages . . . [which] renders these countries distinguished for the talent of improvisation."[12] As Fischlin and Heble note in their introduction to *The Other Side of Nowhere,* encoded within these statements is an incipient "ethnic othering in which the consistent association between improvisatory discourse and Latin/Mediterranean cultures are implicitly opposed to Anglo-Saxon culture."[13]

By the early twentieth century, this process of musical and cultural othering took on new dimensions, especially in North America, where improvisation came to be identified increasingly with African American expressive culture, further reinforcing the divide between improvisation and composition, as well as their perceived class and race affiliations. This constructed—and profoundly false—binary persisted well into the twentieth century, being actively maintained by a variety of institutional contexts surrounding the music, notably university music departments and institutionalized forms of music education more generally.

Things began to change, however, by the middle of the twentieth century as musical improvisation began to reenter Western art music. A variety of factors contributed to this reemergence, including the desire among composers of experimental music for new sounds and new methods of sound production, including those that could not be notated using traditional Western notation. In addition, recording technology may have played a role. In much the same way that technological innovations (namely the ability to produce sheet music) contributed to the demise of improvisation in Western art music more than a century earlier, the invention and eventual widespread circula-tion of sound-recording technologies may well have contributed to the reemergence of musical improvisation in that they allowed improvised musical performances to be recorded, evaluated, circulated, and sold. Pauline Oliveros's description of her first foray into group improvisa-tion supports this idea. She recalls:

> My first group improvisations were with Terry Riley and Loren Rush in 1957. There were no models; there were no scenes for improvisations as there are today. Gathering three composers of concert music to improvise together was unprecedented. Terry had to compose a five-minute film score. He didn't have time to write it so we went to Radio KPFA in Berkeley where Loren was working and recorded several five-minute improvisations for Terry to use for the film soundtrack. Terry selected a track and used it very successfully. We were so interested in the results that we decided to meet again and improvise for fun.[14]

Of particular interest is the role that recording technology played in this historic encounter, one of the first documented instances of modern free improvisation outside of a jazz context. By recording their group improvisations, Oliveros, Riley, and Rush were able to listen back to their improvised musical creations, analyze and evaluate them, and choose the one that best suited their needs at the time.

In the years since, recording technology has become a powerful learn-ing and creative tool for many improvisers working in diverse contexts. In the case of Italian composer/improviser Giacinto Scelsi, the practice of recording improvisations was central to his musical output. Beginning in the early 1950s, Scelsi recorded his own solo improvisations, many of which were performed on the Ondiola, an electronic keyboard instru-ment capable of producing different timbres, glissandi, and microtones. He then hired musicians and composers, notably Vieri Tosatti, to tran-scribe and orchestrate his recorded improvisations.[15] This manner of working destabilizes the ontological status of composition and improvi-sation in thought-provoking ways, and highlights the important connec-tion between recording technology and the reemergence of improvisa-tion in Western art music.

Other musical and cultural factors were at play in this reemergence, including increased contact between musical traditions and systems of musical logic from previously disparate cultural and social locations. Indeed, current conceptions of improvisation in the West are largely the result of the encounter between two streams of music and culture in particular, one with roots in the African diaspora and another with roots in European art music. Despite the widespread vitriol toward jazz and other forms of African American expressive culture in the opening decades of the twentieth century and the fact that many elite-supported cultural institutions (including universities) had willfully ignored those forms for the first half of the twentieth century, modern jazz posed significant challenges to the musical and cultural status quo. There is considerable evidence to suggest that those challenges did not go unnoticed by composers rooted in the Western art music tradition, who began to leave increasingly substantive musical decisions to the discretion of the performers of their works. A clear example of the tendency toward improvisation can be found in the development of graphic scores in the 1950s and 1960s, pieces of music that eschewed traditional forms of notation in favor of diagrammatic musical instructions involving varying degrees of abstraction. Graphic scores placed a great deal of creative agency on the part of performers and played an important role in the reintroduction of musical improvisation into the tradition of Western art music.

In his important essay titled "Improvised Music since 1950: Afrological and Eurological Perspectives," George Lewis convincingly argues that the reemergence of improvisation in Western art music was, in part, a response to improvisatory musical traditions emanating largely from African American communities historically. His insights are worth quoting at length:

> Already active in the 1940s, a group of radical young black American improvisers, for the most part lacking access to economic and political resources often taken for granted in high-culture musical circles, nonetheless posed potent challenges to Western notions of structure, form, communication, and expression. These improvisers, while cognizant of Western musical tradition, located and centered their modes of musical expression within a stream emanating largely from African and African-American cultural and social history. The international influence and dissemination of their music, as well as the strong influences coming from later forms of "jazz," has resulted in the emergence of new sites for transnational, transcultural improvisative musical activity. In particular, a strong circumstantial case can be made for the proposition that the emergence of these new, vigorous, and highly influential improvisative forms provided an impetus for musical workers in other traditions, particularly European and

American composers active in the construction of a transnational European-based tradition, to come to grips with some of the implications of musical improvisation.[16]

The reemergence of real-time modes of music making, by which we mean improvisation and cognate musical processes such as indeterminacy and aleatoricism, represents one of the most significant developments in Western musical discourse over the past half century. Contemporary composers and performers working in a wide variety of musical and cultural locations, both inside the academy and out, have embraced improvisatory approaches to music making. In some cases, like those of Giacinto Scelsi and Lukas Foss, composers have used improvisation as part of their compositional methodology. Many others, including John Cage, Earl Brown, Christian Wolff, Cornelius Cardew, Anthony Braxton, Pauline Oliveros, R. Murray Schafer, and Wadada Leo Smith, have created graphic scores that combine compositional and improvisational elements. Some creative practitioners, including many associated with the Fluxus movement of the 1960s and 1970s, incorporated improvisation into an interdisciplinary and intermedial field of artistic activities. For many musicians, including Derek Bailey, Evan Parker, George Lewis, Maggie Nicols, William Parker, and Joëlle Léandre, to name only a very few, improvisation is a significant and important mode of musical activity in its own right that deserves public recognition and support. Unfortunately, the music curriculum at most North American colleges and universities has not remained in step with these new musical developments. Despite the notable exceptions cited at the outset of this chapter, academic appointments for improvisers remain relatively uncommon, and the vast majority of university courses on musical improvisation continue to focus on improvisation within specific idioms, jazz in particular, rather than on free improvisation or pan-idiomatic forms.

Despite the lag in music performance curricula with respect to improvised music, academic interest in improvisation has increased significantly. A few scholars, notably Bruno Nettl, have written important essays on the subject of improvisation since the 1970s.[17] In the late 1990s, several improvisation-focused colloquia advanced academic interest in, and conversations about, improvisation. Since 1996, as we noted in our previous chapter, the Guelph Jazz Festival Colloquium has been bringing together scholars, creative practitioners, and audiences for vibrant and inspired critical exchanges. Although improvisation had been an important feature in the early iterations of the Guelph Jazz Festival Colloquium, the theme was explicitly signaled and highlighted in the 1998 edition of the event. Titled "The Other Side of Nowhere: Jazz, Improvisation, and Cultural Theory," the 1998 colloquium proved to be particularly significant in building the field of improvisation studies. It provided an early and important networking opportunity for scholars with shared interests who hailed from different places, and who had been working largely in isolation because of institutional structures that reinforced a narrow sense of disciplinarity. In short, the colloquium provided an institutional model that facilitated scholarly mobility and enabled international and intercultural face-to-face networking and community-building. Many of the participants from that colloquium also published revised versions of their papers in the 2004 book *The Other Side of Nowhere: Jazz, Improvisation, and Communities in Dialogue*. In 1999, the year following the Guelph event, a conference titled "Improvising across Borders: An Interdisciplinary Symposium on Improvised Music Traditions" was organized at the University of California, San Diego by, among others, improvising pianist Dana Reason, who was a graduate student there at the time, and who had been one of the presenters at the 1998 Guelph Jazz Festival Colloquium.

One of the interesting things about the participants in these symposia, and about the emergent field of improvisation studies more generally, is the fact that relatively few scholars of improvised music come from a disciplinary background in music. David Borgo has suggested that within the academy historically, jazz has been "too 'Other' for musicology and not 'Other' enough for ethnomusicology."[18] This has been largely true in the case of musical improvisation as well. As a result, scholars hailing from a wide variety of disciplinary backgrounds have contributed to the study of improvisation in important ways.

A case in point is the Improvisation, Community and Social Practice research project (ICASP for short) with which we have been centrally involved. This international research project includes academics hailing from disciplines including not only music, but also anthropology, sociology, cultural studies, race and ethnic studies, gender and women's studies, philosophy, performance studies, English literature, law, French, and more. In 2007, the ICASP project received a $2.5 million Major Collaborative Research Initiative grant from the Social Sciences and Humanities Research Council of Canada that has funded a variety of interrelated research projects on improvisation over the seven-year duration of the award. In addition to several books on the subject of musical improvisation, the ICASP project has spawned many journal articles on improvisation, over twenty colloquia at three Canadian universities, and three intensive summer institutes for graduate students. Over the life of the grant, the project funded over two hundred graduate research positions and seventeen postdoctoral fellowships related to the study of improvisation.

In addition to its activities inside the university environment, ICASP developed improvisation-focused initiatives in conjunction with a variety of not-for-profit community partners. These initiatives have included improvisation workshops with disadvantaged youth, with individuals experiencing homelessness and poverty, and with children with physical and developmental disabilities. Some of these initiatives are discussed in the following chapter. The ICASP team has also developed a series of online resources for educators wishing to incorporate improvisation in their classroom.[19] In addition, ICASP maintains the online peer-reviewed academic journal *Critical Studies in Improvisation / Études critiques en improvisation* published twice a year. Through all of these activities, the ICASP project has played a significant role in shaping the field of improvisation studies and in forging new interdisciplinary relationships between improvisation and the academy.

In 2014, ICASP completed the final year of its seven-year funding cycle. However, in its wake (and building on the momentum that it generated), a partnered research institute known as the International Institute for Critical Studies in Improvisation (IICSI) was established in 2013, receiving another seven-year $2.5 million grant through the Social Sciences and Humanities Research Council of Canada. Like its predecessor, the institute involves an international research team, this time made up of more than fifty scholars from twenty institutions, as well as over thirty community partners. The institute stands at the heart of successful efforts by members of the research team to develop critical studies in improvisation as a new, internationally recognized academic discipline. Its research results—including innovations in adaptive technologies, web platforms and apps for musical improvisation, critical theory, manuals and tool kits for practitioners in social services, rehabilitation therapy, music instruction, and community arts—have been broadly shared via *Critical Studies in Improvisation / Études critiques en improvisation*, a research-intensive website, several international conferences per year, a book series, numerous outreach activities, and hundreds of peer-reviewed publications. A dedicated new state-of-the-art performance and research facility, ImprovLab, is being built as we write this chapter. Moreover, IICSI has recently launched a new interdisciplinary MA and PhD program in critical studies in improvisation at the University of Guelph. With the first full cohort of students having joined us in fall 2019, the initiative draws on faculty expertise across five other partner university sites, and focuses on the development of broader-level skills (for example, collaboration across multiple institutions/organizations and disciplines; internships and community placements; partnership development opportunities; intercultural engagement) with an eye to forming and deploying the skills that lead to both academic and nonacademic employment. The interdisciplinary curriculum seeks to build competency in research, creative practice, and teaching across the following areas: the critical historicization of improvised art and practice; research methods and core concepts in critical studies in improvisation; the development of ethical frameworks for collaborative, community-engaged initiatives; and the development and implementation of practice-based research initiatives—research that recognizes and employs artistic practices both as containing/transmitting knowledges and as a means toward discovering and mobilizing new knowledges. In describing the ICASP and IICSI projects, we have sought to summarize some key scholarly, pedagogical, and creative outputs associated with these initiatives as evidence that a major shift is taking place in the relationship between improvisation and the academy.

We see further evidence of this shift in the work of our colleagues at the International Society for Improvised Music (ISIM). In a message on the organization's website, ISIM founder Ed Sarath tells us, "We have entered an extraordinarily exciting time in the history of music, when musicians have access to an unprecedented expanse of influences and creative strategies. While improvisation in one form or another is increasingly central to this global synthesis, a significant gap looms between the improvisation-based aesthetic paradigm that guides musical practice, and the aesthetic awareness that prevails in the music industry, academic musical world, and society at large." Founded in 2005, ISIM works to promote performance, education, and research in improvised music, organizes international conferences, and, in Sarath's words, "brings together artists, listeners, teachers, critics, scholars, and industry leaders to celebrate the unifying power of improvisation in music and beyond."[20]

The idea of celebrating the power of improvisation in music *and beyond* is also a core part of the work of both ICASP and IICSI. Underpinning both of these initiatives is a recognition of the social instrumentality of improvisational musical practices, the ideal that musical improvisation can serve as "a crucial model for political, cultural, and ethical dialogue and action," to quote from the ICASP website. Similarly, the tagline of an article published to announce the launch of IICSI states that the institute will "explore improvisation as key to world harmony." These are laudable sentiments that we are invested in (and, indeed, at least partially responsible for). But we are also inclined to raise some questions about them. This is not a case of biting the academic hand that feeds, but rather a self-reflexive critical engagement with the discourses surrounding the ICASP and IICSI projects—and surrounding improvisation studies more generally—with a view of understanding more fully the changing relationship(s) between improvisation and the academy.

Despite our own proclamations about the potentially transformative force and critical edge of improvised music, we are the first to admit that improvised modes of musical discourse do not always function in a utopian manner. Improvising ensembles are often rife with power asymmetries that operate under the guise of supposed musical freedom. Whether it is intentional or not, improvising musicians frequently make musical choices that have the effect of silencing other members of an improvising group. In our experiences as performers and educators, we have found that such musical deployments of power often fall along gender lines or other forms of difference. It is important that we exert critical pressure on the utopian ideals that underpin some of the discourse surrounding the ICASP and IICSI projects. They are certainly worth striving for, but they should not blind us to the complex nuances and power dynamics that are always involved in musical performance, improvisatory or otherwise.

We also worry about the effects of increased institutionalization on improvisation, a mode of music making that has valued innovation and risk taking historically and has developed and thrived creatively in large part because it has operated outside of dominant institutional contexts. In his essay "Teaching Improvised Music: An Ethnographic Memoir," George Lewis suggests, indeed, that "a good way to start a heated debate among experienced improvisors is to pose the question of whether improvisation 'can be taught'—a question which, as often as not, refers to the kind of pedagogy associated with schools."[21] Lewis contextualizes the terms of the debate this way: "As the study of improvisative modes of musicality, regardless of tradition, has begun to assume a greater role in the music departments of a number of major institutions of higher learning, it is to be expected that the nature, necessity, and eventual function of such pedagogy would be scrutinized—and eventually contested—from a variety of standpoints, both inside and outside the academy."[22] What happens, then, when improv goes to school? Our chapter title here deliberately riffs on Dave Brubeck's 1954 album of the same name to provoke debate and to call attention to the dangers of musical institutionalization. In this regard, we see modern jazz—notably bebop and its derivatives—as a cautionary tale. To be sure, the increased institutional acceptance of jazz over the past half century or so has had many positive effects: it has given many musicians access to the obvious economic advantages that go along with academic appointments and increased institutional visibility, and it has equipped many young musicians with a very high level of musicianship. But it has also come at a cost: in many respects, the institutionalization of jazz has had a reifying effect on the music, minimizing the emphasis on innovation and musical freedom that has animated jazz from its earliest days. We worry that a similar process of reification could happen to musical improvisation more generally as more and more improvisatory modes of musical discourse are welcomed into the academy as objects of study. We take some comfort in the fact that much of the academic work that is being done on improvisation—through the ICASP and IICSI projects, and, indeed, more generally—is not taking place solely in music departments, but rather in a wide variety of disciplinary and—crucially—interdisciplinary contexts. If musical improvisation is to remain (or truly become) "a crucial model for political, cultural, and ethical dialogue and action," it must continue to develop in the spaces between disciplines. It must also, as we will suggest in our next chapter, continue to develop and be nourished in the spaces, places, and broader communities in which we live, work, and play.

The fact that it is now possible to study musical improvisation as a performance practice or as an object of scholarly analysis—or, indeed, as both—is, we feel, particularly worthy of note. It is our contention that studying improvisation from both a performance and an academic perspective opens a broader range of career options; for students, this is an important consideration given that it is often difficult, if not virtually impossible, to make a living as an improvising musician alone. The learning outcomes associated with the study of improvisation within academic settings are likely to include competency in project development and management, and in vital skills such as planning, problem-solving, listening, leadership, and real-time decision-making. Students studying improvisation in academic settings can develop skills and mindsets that will prepare them for a variety of roles in society as leaders and innovators, applying their nuanced expertise in a wide range of academic, arts-based, and community contexts. Furthermore, we firmly believe that studying improvisation as both theory and practice has the potential to make us better scholars *and* better improvisers. Having firsthand playing experience enriches our ability to analyze and understand the nuances of improvised music. Likewise, developing strong critical-thinking skills in relation to improvised musical discourse makes us more attentive to the power dynamics involved in improvised musical interaction as well as the broader social and cultural implications of those dynamics. The ability to speak and write about our own improvisatory creative practice in a lucid way also has advantages—when writing grant applications to support our work, for example.

The idea of studying improvisation from both a theoretical and practical perspective is central to a course that I (Jesse) teach at Carleton University, a course titled Improvisation in Theory and Practice.[23] The course outline states: "This course will examine musical improvisation as both a theoretical practice and a practical theory. In addition to weekly discussion seminars that focus on selected texts drawn from the emergent field of improvisation studies, the class will engage in experiential forms of learning by actively improvising in a weekly performance-oriented seminar." The class meets twice per week. One session is devoted to seminar-style discussions of readings drawn from the field of improvisation studies that examine issues including history/historiography, genre, race, gender, sexuality, and pedagogy as they have intersected with improvisatory musical practices historically. The other half of our time is devoted to improvising with one another, often within a loose set of parameters suggested by me or other members of the group. In both the seminar discussions and playing sessions, the emphasis is on dialogue: all the members of the class are encouraged to voice their ideas. Although the structure of the course seemingly separates the theory and practical components, I emphasize that all of our activities are both theory and practice—whether we are improvising with one another musically or discussing scholarly writing about improvisation.

Students come to the class from a wide variety of musical backgrounds. Some have experience improvising within particular musical genres such as jazz and rock. Students who are steeped in the classical tradition often claim to have no experience with musical improvisation. I suggest otherwise based on the fact that in every mode of music making involving human musicians—even notated and highly prescriptive forms of music—performers routinely make decisions in the course of performance: decisions in response to the acoustics of the room, to the sound or action of a particular instrument, and so on.

Given the diverse musical backgrounds of the students in the course, we generally focus on free improvisation, or what I prefer to think of as "pan-idiomatic improvisation." To quote from the course outline again:

> The performance seminars will focus primarily on so called "free" improvisation—what Derek Bailey has called "non-idiomatic" improvisation; that is, improvised music that does not try to represent a particular musical genre in a sustained way. Instead, we will be free to draw on musical techniques and signifiers derived from virtually *any* musical tradition, incorporating them into the music that we create collaboratively in the moment of performance. In this regard, it is perhaps more accurate to think of our musical activities as constituting a form of "pan-idiomatic" free improvisation rather than "non-idiomatic." Focusing on such modes of musical interaction will provide opportunities for participants to hone their listening skills and expand their musical vocabularies, two transferrable skills that are of obvious value in any musical context.

We record all of our improvising sessions and I make an audio recording of each session available to the members of the class in order to provide opportunities for them to reflect on, and critically engage with, their own playing and that of the class as a whole. Audio recordings cannot really capture the complexities of an improvisatory music performance, offering instead a kind of sonic snapshot of a multilayered experience. Nonetheless, listening to recordings of our own improvisations can be a powerful learning tool, as noted in chapter one.

Grading and evaluation in the course revolve around the following:

1. Participation in class discussions / reading response questions
2. An improv journal in which students reflect on course content, including assigned readings, class discussions, group improvisations, and the recordings of our performance-seminars.
3. A short essay in which students research the history of their own instrument in relation to improvisatory modes of music making
4. A long essay (and proposal) on any topic related to musical improvisation
5. A presentation of an idea for the final group performance
6. The final group performance itself

In my view, if a person really wants to absorb the language of any mode of music making, it is important that he or she listens to—and learns from—the history/histories of that music. As a means to that end, I begin most classes with some listening. I also include a listening list on the course outline with YouTube links to recordings by many improvisers including Derek Bailey, Anthony Braxton, William Parker, Milford Graves, Fred Anderson, Kidd Jordan, Hamid Drake, AMM, Cecil Taylor, Tony Oxley, Alexander von Schlippenbach, Evan Parker, the Globe Unity Orchestra, Instant Composers Pool, Peter Brötzmann, George Lewis, Fred Frith, John Zorn, Muhal Richard Abrams, Roscoe Mitchell, Pauline Oliveros, Irène Schweizer, Joëlle Léandre, Maggie Nicols, Bill Dixon, the Art Ensemble of Chicago, Phil Minton, Butch Morris, Wadada Leo Smith, and others. To encourage members of the class to listen to the assigned recordings, I have added a series of "pop quiz" listening tests to more recent editions of the course.

On a few occasions, students have voiced dissatisfaction about some of the assigned readings in the course and our discussions thereof. Recalling comments referred to in George Lewis's "Teaching Improvised Music" essay, some students ask questions along the lines of "Why can't we just improvise? Why do we have to spend so much time reading about it?" Some students have questioned the emphasis that some of the readings placed on power dynamics within improvisatory modes of music making, and the emphasis on difference along lines of gender, race, sexuality, and the like. In earlier editions of the course, I heard or read statements like these: "Sexism and racism are things of the past. They aren't an issue for our generation. So why do we have to keep talking about them?" One of the effects of statements like this, when they are voiced in class, is to discourage class members who find themselves in minoritized positions to voice their own experiences of discrimination on the bandstand, in the classroom, or in society in general. Several women in the class have expressed discomfort with the masculinist tone of some of the things said in class, but they generally do so privately within the context of their journals. In some cases, they told me that they chose to remain silent in class because they didn't want to gain a negative reputation among their male classmates, thereby running the risk of being further ostracized or otherwise punished for speaking out.

I exert as much critical pressure as possible on masculinist attitudes within the class and on pronouncements concerning the irrelevance of race, class, and gender to the study and performance of improvised music. I also draw attention to the institutional frameworks that have surrounded cultural production and music education historically and the overwhelmingly disproportionate amount of support that modes of music making that have emerged out of European and European-American communities have received when compared to jazz and other forms of improvisatory musics to have emanated primarily out of the African Diaspora. We discuss the problematic—and patently false—racialized taxonomies of improvised music that continue to circulate in many discourses surrounding contemporary music. We discuss privilege—white privilege, male privilege, class privilege, and the like—and discuss some of the ways in which privileges of various kinds play out inside the academy, on the bandstand, and in the wider public sphere.

These conversations are never easy or comfortable. But I consider them to be fundamentally important both to the aims of the class and to the study and performance of musical improvisation. These sorts of power dynamics do continue to exist, shaping both cultural production and knowledge production. We do not do ourselves—or our students—any favors by pretending they don't exist or ignoring them. In some ways, a class on improvisation is uniquely positioned to foster discussions about the negotiation of differences, musical and otherwise, and the cultural politics of music making. But it is important that the discussion doesn't end there. Indeed, we hope that educators working in all facets of the music curriculum—including both performance and musicology courses including those with more canonized institutional and intellectual histories—find opportunities to have these sorts of conversations with their students.

I took some comfort in something that one student wrote in his journal in response to some of the discussions we were having in class. With his permission, we will reprint his comments here. He began by saying, "It is kind of upsetting how many readings we do are focused on inequality," thereby echoing statements that several of his classmates had made. But then he went on to state:

> The passages from this week about gender and improvisation were pretty hard-hitting. I found that as much as I wanted to disagree with the idea that these injustices are present in our daily lives as musicians, I simply couldn't. Prior to this class I've been in group situations where collaborative musical improvisation was taking place between a mixed gendered group and as I look back I can recall times where the female participants were being ignored in certain ways and not given the opportunity to lead the jam. I've seen male musicians interrupt contributions of their female peers. I've even seen certain musicians

of the male variety give hostile looks towards a female musician who is trying to add something different into the sonic mix. When I realized that these issues of gender that we've been discussing in class are very real, it gave me a really terrible feeling. I hope I've never subconsciously contributed to this injustice, but from now on I will certainly be more careful to consider everyone in an improvisatory musical setting before picking up my instrument.

I was pleased to read this statement, which I believe was sincere. Interestingly, I heard a corresponding change in this student's playing around the time that he voiced these ideas. To my ears, he became a better improviser. He listened more attentively; he found ways to support his bandmates musically to a greater extent, even if that meant laying out when his first instinct was to play.

In general, students in recent editions of the Improvisation in Theory and Practice course seem to be more open and receptive to discussions of power, privilege, and difference than they were when the course began. It is possible that this is because word about the course content has traveled among students and they now have a better sense of what they are signing up for when they register for the class. It is also apparent that students have become more aware of the prevalence of sexism and racism in contemporary society thanks in large part to recent social movements including #MeToo and Black Lives Matter. In Canada, the National Inquiry into Missing and Murdered Indigenous Women and Girls and the 2015 release of the Truth and Reconciliation Commission's "94 Calls to Action" aimed at redressing the serious harms caused by the residential school system and creating better relations between the Canadian government and Indigenous nations have drawn attention to the history of colonial violence against Indigenous peoples to a significant extent. These important public conversations have made students more receptive to discussions of privilege, race, class, gender, and sexuality as they relate to the music that we make.

The emergent role of the improviser-academic also raises important questions about power dynamics and academic privilege, and we would be remiss not to take note of these. How, for example, are we to understand the tension between, on the one hand, improvisers who have become tenured faculty members in privileged academic spaces and, on the other, creative practitioners who may sometimes (perhaps even often) struggle to make a living wage in their communities? Though critical studies in improvisation is often seen as a progressive field of inquiry, to what extent does its very institutionalization within elitist academic spaces run the risk of placing it at odds with the lived experiences and the situated knowledges of its practitioners, and with the internal education endeavors of the communities from which the music has emerged? Will a new graduate program, such as the one we've described above, further this distance between academics and communities of artistic practice, or might it (as we are hoping) offer purposeful opportunities to bridge the divide? Do the structures of reward within university settings (such as tenure and promotion) foster an environment in which faculty members too often seek to advance their own careers at the expense of the communities of interest they purport to support and represent? How might improviser-academics best use their privilege and status within the academy to make a difference for those communities? Or, to borrow again from Sara Evans and Harry Boyte, "What are the structures of support, the resources, and the experiences that generate the capacity and inspiration to challenge 'the way things are' and imagine a different world?"[24] In what ways, in short, might the pedagogy of musical improvisation within the academy work to unsettle dominant epistemic orders and contribute to a more just society?

If it is the task and responsibility of intellectuals, as Edward Said has argued, to speak out against injustice and suffering, if "the challenge of intellectual life is to be found in dissent against the status quo when the struggle on behalf of underrepresented and disadvantaged groups seems so unfairly weighted against them,"[25] then how might academic improvisers best respond to and take up this challenge, how might they most purposefully engage in forms of social critique? And are there ways to ensure that such critique, such commitment to critical responsibility, is (and remains) a core concern when improvisation goes to school? In our view, improviser-academics have an opportunity—and a responsibility—to intervene in public (mis)understandings of improvisation, to draw attention to (and be in solidarity with) the work of improvising artists, and to mobilize resources and create opportunities that might not otherwise be available to improvising musicians. If, as the passage from Malcolm Goldstein quoted at the outset of this chapter reminds us, the choices we make about what we do, or do not, teach can be powerful indicators of public value, social inclusion, and cultural legitimacy, then the study of improvisation in the academic classroom is itself an important act of (and site for) meaning-making. George Lewis, as we saw in chapter two, similarly sees in improvisation "a kind of pedagogical relation, in which we listen to know where we are and where the others are; where ideas and information are communicated from each to the other; where one learns about the other through hearing what the other has to play; and where one learns about oneself through listening to the responses from the other that seem somehow to be related to you."[26] At stake, then, when improv goes to school, are vital matters of social commitment, critical listening, co-learning, knowledge mobilization, and public interest. Such matters are equally at stake when the pedagogy of musical improvisation moves beyond the academic classroom into broader communities of practice and involvement.

 | A Force That's Active in the World

Community-Oriented Pedagogies
of Improvisation

The 2007 Guelph Jazz Festival Colloquium celebrated the launch of the recently announced Improvisation, Community, and Social Practice (ICASP) project. During an onstage interview with Amiri Baraka and William Parker, interviewer Ron Gaskin asked Parker if he had any comments to make about the fact that two and a half million dollars of federal funding had recently been allocated in Canada for a research project based on improvisation. Those of us in the audience who were involved with the project were on the edges of our seats as we waited for Parker's response: after all, here was an opportunity for one of the preeminent practitioners of the music on which we had modeled so much of our work to offer us his praise, his blessing, his good wishes. Or so we thought. Instead of congratulating us, however, Parker took the occasion to critique the very notion that improvisation is something that should (or even could) be studied. "People who study birds," he remarked, "can't fly. It's a nice idea, but in the long run it's just an intellectual exercise to say, 'I know what improvisation is.'" If Parker's provocative comments were bound to raise hackles with at least some members of the audience, he didn't stop there: "Now, if you say, okay, with improvisation I can feed the poor. With improvisation I can build housing for the homeless. With improvisation I can build schools for those who don't have schools. Then I might be interested in trying to define improvisation. I think money should be better spent someplace else, personally," he remarked, upping the ante. Parker's comments were important, if controversial, for they opened an ongoing dialogue about a range of issues that are of central importance not only to the ICASP project, but also to the study of improvisation in general: issues surrounding the relationship(s) between theory and practice (to what extent is it necessary for researchers studying musical improvisation to have experience as improvising musicians?); issues of privilege (what does it mean for a group of researchers with academic appointments to study the work of improvising musicians, most of whom have not had access to such appointments historically or the economic benefits that go along with them?); and, crucially, issues of social responsibility (what roles can improvisation play in bettering the lives of poor and disenfranchised communities?).

During the Q and A session that followed the formal interview, our colleague and fellow ICASP research team member Ellen Waterman responded to Parker by noting that our project wasn't created with the aim of trying to discover or define improvisation. Acknowledging that much of the work that Parker and Baraka have done is an important part of the inspiration for the project, Waterman insisted on setting the record straight about the work we sought to do in our communities. Her rejoinder, an example of improvised public dialogue, is worth quoting at length:

> We're not out to define improvisation, dissect it, or put it on the table and vivisect it or something. We want to explore ways in which improvisation is active in the world to create social change. And a lot of our funding in our project is to work with community organizations, whether that is a youth shelter or an inner-city exchange in Vancouver, whether that is artists, collectives . . . to develop projects that really explore the implications of improvisation for larger social ideas. We're really aware of the pitfalls you correctly raise in your criticism, but if we end up writing some abstruse kind of papers about improvisation and we haven't done anything, or we haven't helped anybody, then we would have failed—signally. For me to sleep at night as a university professor, I have to know that the work I'm doing is relevant to young people, that I am helping to prepare young people to make change in our society, and am working towards that change myself. So that is what our project is about, and yeah we got a lot of money from our government—how bizarre is that? That they actually funded people to take seriously radical musical practices that could model ways for people to behave with one another in this world.

Improvisation as a force that's active in the world. Improvisation as a radical musical practice that models ways for people to behave and interact with one another. Improvisation as a potential agent of positive social change. Waterman's comments aptly capture some of what is at stake in our consideration of improvisation as both musical and social practice.[1] One of our central contentions in this book, in fact, is that when we examine both the musical and social implications of improvisation, we're encouraged to recognize the extent to which the teaching of improvisation is about more than just musical instruction. As Waterman's comments suggest, improvisation can be understood—and, indeed, taught—as a valuable tool for building vibrant and resilient communities and for developing active and engaged cultural and political agents. At a time when we are seeing growing interest in, and involvement with, experimental artistic practices, as well as an expanding body of scholarly work in critical pedagogy, there is a significant opportunity to reflect on and analyze the transformative pedagogical power of improvisation and its impact on the communities in which it takes place. Recall Doris Sommer's argument that what often begins as an artistic practice doesn't necessarily stop there, how it can "ripple into extra-artistic institutions and practices," and how humanistic interpretation "has an opportunity to trace those ripple effects and to speculate about the dynamics in order to encourage more movement."[2] Recall our belief that the future of the field of critical studies in improvisation resides, at least in part, in our capacity to encourage and to track such movement, and to consider how the improvisational practices of artists and the educational endeavors of community groups might enable generative new forms of community-making, critical thinking, and social practice.

In some sense, William Parker's suggestion that "people who study birds can't fly" ought to remind us that discussion about whether or not improvisation is something that can be effectively taught is bound to continue, and that the terms of the debate will continue to be up for grabs. In our view, thoughtful reflection and respectful dialogue about such comments and their underlying assumptions offer valuable learning opportunities for students and teachers of improvisation. Indeed, engaging in such dialogue is a vital step in the kind of field-developing and community-building that enables the activist pedagogical interventions that interest us.

The activist orientation that Waterman correctly describes as animating much of our work aligns with many of the arguments that have been made about "community music." In his book *Community Music: In Theory and in Practice,* Lee Higgins suggests that one way to understand community music is "as an approach to active music making and musical knowing *outside* of formal teaching and learning situations. By *formal*, I mean music that is delivered by professionals in schools, colleges, and other statutory organizations through formalized curricula."[3] With community music, he goes on to explain, "there is an emphasis on people, participation, context, equality of opportunity, and diversity. Musicians who work in this way seek to create relevant and accessible music-making experiences that integrate activities such as listening, improvising, musical invention, and performing."[4] In this chapter, we take a look at some examples of community-oriented improvisation pedagogies with which we have been directly involved that have taken place outside of formal teaching and learning situations. These case studies provide a showcase for a wide range of activities that, we believe, demonstrate the power, impact, and effectiveness of improvisational pedagogies as a force that is "active in the world."

Through an analysis of the examples on which we draw (and the partnerships that have enabled them), we seek to open up a conversation about the impact that improvising musicians and educators can have in the communities in which they work. We mention partnerships here because we want to stress their importance; we want to emphasize that they need to be a key part of the conversation, especially in the context of community-based music-making. Indeed, we're mindful of George Lewis's suggestion that one of the most pressing concerns on the research agenda for scholars working on issues related to improvisation and pedagogy is to ask, "What kinds of new theoretical and organizational models, as well as new practices, can be developed for the creation and nurturing of itinerant-institutional partnerships for the teaching of improvisation, the development of improvisation teachers, and theories of education that embed improvisation itself as a methodology?"[5] Our case studies suggest that a particularly effective way of facilitating such improvisational pedagogies involves the establishment and nurturing of what Lewis refers to as "itinerant-institutional partnerships." The benefits of such partnerships are reciprocal and multiple: they serve to break down barriers between different communities (including those between the academy and the wider public sphere), enabling different people from diverse backgrounds to engage in a productive and cocreative process of dialogue and knowledge exchange. Part of what's at issue, then, is the importance of diversifying the range of educational principles and concepts involved in pedagogies of improvisation, as well as the range of participants and the base of valued knowledges therein. Two interrelated educational philosophies that hold great potential for the teaching and learning of improvisation (and have influenced our own approach to the subject in crucial ways) are (1) the field of critical pedagogy and (2) the principles and priorities articulated in the United Nations World Program of Human Rights Education.

One of the central tenets of critical pedagogy is the idea that students must be active agents in their own process of learning, developing a critical consciousness that will enable them to recognize and challenge unjust power relations and to work toward a more just society. When it comes to music education, we believe that the study of improvisation provides a unique opportunity to critically examine and transform unequal power dynamics in the classroom, on the bandstand, and within the wider communities in which we live, work, and learn. Recall Henry Giroux's suggestion that pedagogy needs to be understood not just in terms of the transmission of knowledge within classrooms, but more broadly as "the complicated processes by which knowledge is produced, skills are learned meaningfully, identities are shaped, desires are mobilized, and critical dialogue becomes a central form of public interaction."[6] The United Nations World Program of Human Rights Education offers a related claim: "Introducing or improving human rights education in the school system," it explains, "requires adopting a holistic approach to teaching and learning by integrating program objectives and content, resources, methodologies, assessment, and evaluation by *looking beyond the classroom and by building partnerships*."[7] While not all community-oriented improvisation pedagogies will necessarily or explicitly take up questions of social justice or human rights, the United Nations World Program of Human Rights Education's assessment of a holistic approach to teaching and learning has informed our approach to the pedagogy of musical improvisation, and that of several researchers associated with the ICASP project and the IICSI.

In conjunction with a number of community partners (including social service organizations and music festivals) across numerous sites associated with ICASP and IICSI, members of the ICASP and IICSI research teams have designed and implemented a series of ongoing community-engagement initiatives in which improvisation plays a central role. As the following case studies suggest, community partnerships involving musical improvisation can teach us vital lessons about wider social issues such as the development and maintenance of healthy communities, the negotiation of difference, and the formation of identities. In discussing these partnerships, we certainly do not wish to objectify the community partners and/or participants with whom we have collaborated. Rather, we want to discuss our experiences openly and reflexively in order to share some of the things we have learned and to provide a set of ideas, models, tools, and resources that we hope will be of value to other educators who are similarly committed to community-focused pedagogies of musical improvisation.

Play Who You Are: Learning from a Decade of Community-Based Improvisation

Launched initially by the ICASP initiative in two cities in summer 2008, the Play Who You Are: Improvisation, Pedagogy, and Community project began as a partnership between the Guelph Jazz Festival and the KidsAbility Centre for Child Development in Guelph, and between the Suoni Per Il Popolo Festival and Head and Hands / À Deux Mains in Montreal. Through the festivals, we were able to secure funding from the Canada Council for the Arts' Artists and Community Collaboration program to hold workshops and concerts with youth in both cities.

Through the partnership with KidsAbility, we've been bringing world-class improvising musicians into creative collaboration with children and youth with disabilities. The musician-facilitators lead workshops that help to develop the youths' musical skills, confidence, and repertoires, and the group works together to stage a public performance during the Guelph Jazz Festival. Ongoing research by members of our team has explored a range of topics, including the short- and long-term impacts of improvised arts participation; pedagogical approaches to teaching improvised music in community settings; the therapeutic role of improvised creative practices; and the impact of improvisation programming on community cohesion. We've seen firsthand through this work how improvisation enables new models of cooperation, adaptation, and listening within at-risk populations, and how it fosters vibrant, cohesive, resilient communities, while increasing self-esteem, self-confidence, leadership, and social skills.

KidsAbility is a community-based social service organization that provides children and young adults (birth to eighteen years of age) who have developmental, physical, and communication disabilities, with appropriate educational, physical, and socioemotional support. It is a local branch of a larger provincial unit, serving a medium-sized urban center (and surrounding rural areas) in south-central Ontario, Canada. Its services range from occupational therapy and physiotherapy to social work and therapeutic recreation, as well as assessment, consultation, parental support/education, equipment recommendations, and regular monitoring. Empowering children and youth with disabilities to recognize their full potential by working together with families, schools, and community groups is the organization's main focus.

When we launched the Play Who You Are initiative with KidsAbility, it was with a series of five workshops and a concert that brought together youth, staff, and parents with improvising musicians, the Guelph Jazz Festival, and a team of researchers. A preliminary workshop was held early in July 2008 in order to introduce the kids to the idea of improvisation and to assess their interest. Subsequent workshops were held on two weekends in late August and early September, culminating in a performance at the Guelph Jazz Festival during the festival's biggest outdoor event. We tracked the work through research conducted by our students. Research was gathered through participant observation; open-ended, semistructured interviews with the staff, young people, parents, and artist facilitators; exit surveys; and video recordings. We also recorded the participants' final performance at the Guelph Jazz Festival.[8]

Fast-forward to September 2017, when we celebrated ten years of the Play Who You Are research-outreach initiative. During the 2017 edition of the Guelph Jazz Festival and the related conference that takes place as a core part of the festival's schedule of activities, we showcased and disseminated our findings after a decade of this collaborative inquiry from Play Who You Are, bringing into dialogue ten years of research, participants, and data. By convening artist facilitators, participants, researchers, community members, and practitioners to reflect on their involvement with the Play Who You Are initiative, we had a rare and important opportunity to engage in interactive, longitudinal analysis of our practices, impacts, and pathways for future learning.[9]

Research on arts-based community-making has to date focused on topics ranging from aesthetic contexts[10] to impacts related to social justice and social change,[11] to information and knowledge about public health.[12] Recent research also includes an emphasis on personal growth, agency, and transformation.[13] However, as Joshua Guetzkow notes, longitudinal studies on the impact of the arts on communities, though desirable, tend to be very rare.[14] Through our ten-year research partnership with KidsAbility, we have been able to explore how (and to what extent) improvisational arts-based practices contribute to the development and flourishing of healthy communities over the long term.

Building from Alex Lubet's contention that "to deny access to participation in music . . . is literally dehumanizing,"[15] the Play Who You Are project creates opportunities for inclusion, collaboration, and recognition through community improvisation across ages and abilities. There exists a lively field of research and dialogue about music education, community music and arts, and the links between arts participation and well-being (whether mental, physical, or community health). Inspired by Lee Higgins's understanding of community music as a practice "that promotes . . . participation, opportunity, and diversity" and encourages participants to "dream of a politics of, and for, a musical future that is marked with active and meaningful participation,"[16] we have sought to expand the scope of this body of research to focus on the complex interactions and combined impacts of community engagement, practice-based research methodologies, and musical improvisation.

From the research we've conducted, it's clear to us that the Play Who You Are initiative has gone some distance in enabling participants to realize the "dream of . . . meaningful participation." Reflecting on some of the findings and impacts of the project over its ten-year history, KidsAbility staff member Heather Granger—a recreation therapist who has been our primary point of contact with the organization for most of the last decade, and who has been central to the design, implementation, dissemination, and evaluation of our partnered research—spoke about participation in community as a central objective of her work: "When we look at our services and the partnerships and where we're going to put our efforts," she explained, "we look for things that are going to engage our clients and help them build the skills they need to be participating in community." She and others during that panel discussion commented on the ways in which meaningful participation has been built during the Play Who You Are project. From her perspective as a clinical therapist, Granger stressed how important it is that "improvisation is really an accessible point of entry for participants. It's inherently collaborative in nature and it can be approached with no musical background." She reminded us that "some of the participants come with no musical experience, no identification with being on stage or being a professional [musician]. . . . That in itself is a huge opportunity and a huge self-esteem builder for a lot of participants."

It is clear to us that the impacts of the workshops and performances have been numerous, with research we've been conducting over the years repeatedly highlighting several key themes, including increased self-esteem, self-expression, and self-confidence, increased ability to listen and focus, and a sense of group cohesion. In our interviews after the initial iteration of the Play Who You Are project in 2008, for example, one mother stated, "I think the hugest thing might even just be building anyone's self-esteem. . . . I think that's important."[17] Over the years, we have heard many stories and memories of how the workshops and performances have drawn out shy kids who were initially reluctant to join in the activities. Here's a memorable example from the first year of the project:

> One boy who had no previous experience with music, and who was extremely shy and withdrawn, fell in love with the clamorous sound of the kitchen sink [one of the homemade instruments], (in fact, he could hardly refrain from beating it repeatedly!), and emerged from his shyness to become more engaged with the group. As his father noted, through playing the kitchen sink, his son had the opportunity to increase his self-confidence, and even began looking up during the workshops (a real achievement for him). Recognizing this transformation, the workshop facilitators celebrated the noise and the student's new level of engagement. A young volunteer creatively employed sign language to help the boy know when to stop and go, thus managing what could have seemed a disruptive noise level.[18]

In addition to increased self-esteem, many Play Who You Are participants have shown increased self-confidence. Drawing again from research conducted during the first iteration of the project, we noted how

> participants' self-confidence was . . . demonstrated through their conducting the rest of the group. Every child had the opportunity to conduct (though some chose not to). One boy, who conducted at the final concert, told us that being able to lead was his favourite part of the workshop experience: "I like how I can actually be the boss and go like, 'Do this, do that, this, that. Do this, do that.' I'm tired of people always ordering me around all the time." We also learned that one of the older girls who conducted had never before chosen to get up in front of a group in any activity. As one volunteer noted, people with special needs "don't have a lot of opportunities to be a leader. . . . So having a chance to be up there and stand in front of everyone, and find that people are following them and listening to them . . . [boosted the participants'] self-confidence." Finally, as another girl's mother shared with us, she was surprised that her daughter had such confidence to get up and conduct the group: "I wasn't sure how she was going to be with that . . . I thought she was just going to stand,

being totally lost. But she absorbed, even though at some point it didn't seem that she was listening and watching, she absorbed what the instructions were." The opportunity to conduct proved to be an important component of the workshop by providing a leadership role (an uncommon occurrence for youth with special needs), as well as the opportunity to practice what they had learned during the workshops and to add individual variations and style.[19]

If this notion of spontaneous leadership was celebrated as an important achievement during the first iteration of the Play Who You Are initiative in 2008, it continues to be a defining feature of the project a decade later. In this context, Heather Granger's comments from the 2017 panel discussion are, again, worth quoting. Noting how "spontaneous leadership really evolves out of . . . group dynamics," she hinted at how improvisation functions as a form of anticipatory behavior, how, as a strategy for action, it trains and enables participants to understand the environment in which they find themselves and to recognize how your actions might shape things, might have an impact on what will happen next: in Granger's words, to "see that I have the power to make music and to lead the group in what the sound is going to be." This kind of leadership, for Granger, "is a really key part of this project."

Granger's comments about the ability of participants to recognize how the choices they make will shape "what the sound is *going to be*" suggest that improvisation cultivates a form of intuitively anticipatory behavior: the ability to recognize and anticipate what will happen next, and to act accordingly. The implications of this form of behavior are potentially far-reaching. As another researcher with a deep history of involvement with the Play Who You Are initiative, Elizabeth Jackson, puts it: "The hope of this project lies in those moments where we're not just managing . . . but we're creating alternative power relations, alternative forms of communication, ways of knowing that are deeply intimate, powerful, unconventional and therefore, have great potential."[20]

For participants, one of the key factors contributing to these alternative models of communication and ways of knowing has been the ability to focus and listen deeply. In our panel discussion reflecting on our decade of research findings, a number of panelists spoke about the importance of how the workshops and performances have helped participants to become better and more curious listeners. Heather Granger noted the kind of "deep listening that . . . requires a very accepting and trusting relationship, [that] requires participants to take a lot of risks."

And throughout the workshops over the years, we've noted that participants have developed the impressive ability to focus and rehearse—often for a continuous hour and a half, which according to the staff and parents, was a rare occurrence for these youth—while simultaneously listening to the artists and to each other. Despite the fact that the room in which the workshops took place contained several researchers and many parents and staff, the players stayed intent on and engaged with their musical activities, a concentration that has extended to the final public performance. Not wishing to force this public performance component on the children, we had emphasized through our initial exploratory discussions with KidsAbility the workshops as a fun chance to participate in improvisational music, an end in itself, with the concert as an optional extra, should the participants be interested. Yet, surprising to our team, all of the kids and their parents were excited about being part of the concert, were motivated to prepare for it, and did not seem fazed by the unfamiliar situation of being on stage in front of thousands of people, amid equipment, technicians, and a sizable audience. As one parent explained, he thought that the relaxed and unpressured atmosphere created by the artist facilitators allowed the young people not only to gain the confidence to perform in public, but also to focus intently on their music making: during the performance "they were really more themselves, and you know, they were able to focus." In the end, the final performance during that first iteration of the program, but also in each of the subsequent years throughout our decade-long partnership, went extremely well and was positively received. The youthful performers not only showed tremendous confidence, but they also displayed great listening and focus skills throughout the performance.[21]

The impact of this work goes far beyond the scholarly realm. Comments we've received over the years from parents, youth, staff, and creative practitioners make clear that these activities play a role in helping to foster vibrant, cohesive communities within at-risk urban youth populations. One parent, Amy Baskin, whose daughter Talia participated in the Play Who You Are initiative, responded to our partnership activities with KidsAbility by writing in a blog for *Today's Parent* magazine: "We who parent children with disabilities don't get many opportunities to see our kids shine like that." She continues: "We celebrated the kids as they are—perfect and beautiful and full of rhythm and song. In front of a huge crowd, the kids played piano, shakers, slide whistles and drums. Talia [her daughter] smiled confidently as she took centre stage to sing and to play. And, autism or no autism, this girl positively glowed."[22]

Indeed, another key impact of the workshops has been a lesson for us, as researchers, in learning from children and youth—in this particular case, from young people with physical and developmental challenges who, along with the parents and teachers who work with them everyday, have taught us transformational lessons about adaptation, playfulness, and grace.

Another parent, Barbara Sellers, summarized the impact of her daughter Katy's involvement with the Play Who You Are initiative, this way:

> The Jazz Improv project was truly innovative and I, as a parent of a special needs child, would venture to say was pretty risky. One could never have seen the end from the beginning. [The project] brought children and youth, who have communication, behavioural, and other significant physical and/or developmental challenges, together with ground-breaking musicians to make music together in venues all around our city—out there flying without a net. Not only was our kids' engagement with the musicians amazing to witness, but also the community response to the music they made together was truly heart-warming. I will always remember, despite the barriers, seeing the connections being made, which went way beyond words, way beyond any of our expectations.
>
> Katy's PDD-Autism will continue to present her with significant challenges in life and for participation in community. But these early inclusive experiences, communicating through music and participating in the process of making joyful sounds in community together with others, have given her, and so many others like her, something very strong to build upon. Perhaps more importantly, [this] work has helped take us forward by leaps and bounds towards a more inclusive, barrier free community. Thank you from the bottom of my heart.[23]

As part of our ten-year celebration of the Play Who You Are initiative and in an effort to showcase our research, we commissioned two new short films titled *Stories of Impact*, featuring the Play Who You Are alumni to whom we've referred here, Talia and Katy. The films were screened in September 2017 at the Guelph Jazz Festival Colloquium, "Partnering for Change: Learning outwards from Jazz and Improvisation," in front of the colloquium audience, which included parents, families, youth, and staff from KidsAbility, as well as our international conference delegates. Both Talia and Katy, who have been participants in the Play Who You

Are initiative over the course of several years, were in attendance for the screening.[24]

Based on the successes of the Play Who You Are workshops and performances, we have made this project an annual collaboration, bringing KidsAbility youth together with other artists/teachers who work with the kids over several sessions to produce a culminating concert at the Guelph Jazz Festival.[25] We continue to gather data through participant observation, annual interviews with the participants, staff, parents, and workshop facilitators, and audio-video documentation of workshops and performances. ICASP/IICSI researchers have developed similarly collaborative community-oriented improvisational programs in Montreal (with Head and Hands), in Vancouver (through the Carnegie Centre in Vancouver's Downtown Eastside), and in Ottawa through Carleton University and the We Are All Musicians project.

We Are All Musicians:
Reflections on *Mud Lake Symphony* and *Turning the Page*

We Are All Musicians (WAAM) is an interdisciplinary research-creation project I (Jesse) started in 2012. The guiding philosophy behind the project is the idea that music is a fundamental human right: everyone deserves to have opportunities to make music, regardless of their level of musical training, income, age, or level of physical/cognitive ability. In order to realize this vision, the WAAM project uses a variety of innovative "adaptive use" and "movement to music" technologies in conjunction with more traditional musical instruments to foster improvisatory musical interaction in an inclusive way, particularly among individuals and communities that have experienced barriers to making music historically, notably children and adults living in low-income situations, and individuals with disabilities of various kinds.

The primary objectives behind the WAAM project are these:

1. To create truly inclusive environments for group music-making, environments that respect and celebrate differences of various kinds: musical, physical, cognitive, social, cultural, gender, etc.
2. To study the social processes and social effects of inclusive music-making and the musical negotiation of difference
3. To develop new models and new technologies for inclusive, community-oriented music-making and to refine existing models and technologies

4. To disseminate knowledge about inclusive music-making through publications, presentations, workshops, performances, and audio and video recordings
5. To create and stage a series of aesthetically compelling collaborative public performances that put into practice the ideals, concepts, and technologies associated with the WAAM project

In the pages that follow, I discuss three WAAM collaborations: one with a group of schoolchildren, one with a group of artists with disabilities, and one with seniors with Alzheimer's and other forms of dementia, as well as their caregivers.

Despite the growing body of evidence that shows that studying music has significant benefits for children's intellectual, social, and emotional development and well-being,[26] support for music education in the Ontario public education system—and in many other jurisdictions—has diminished over the past several decades. The rationale, we are told, is that reducing music and arts education will leave more time for teachers and students to focus on subjects related to STEM disciplines (science, technology, engineering, and math)—in other words, those subjects that are perceived to more readily prepare students for the workforce. Increasingly, music education has come to be regarded as the responsibility of parents who must provide music instruction for their children through private lessons. Unfortunately, this downloading of music education from the public education system onto parents means that low-income families are at a distinct disadvantage when it comes to providing music lessons for their children. A case in point is Regina Street Alternative School (previously Regina Street Public School), where I was invited to be the artist-in-residence during the 2013–2014 school year.

Regina Street Alternative School (RSAS) is a school for children in junior kindergarten to grade 6 in the west end of Ottawa. In most public schools in Ontario, music instruction begins in earnest in grade 7. Therefore, RSAS does not have a music teacher or music program. Of the school's roughly 160 students, many of whom came from disadvantaged backgrounds, fewer than 5 received private music lessons at the time I started going to the school. Many RSAS parents simply do not have the financial resources to pay for private music lessons for their children. This pattern of unequal access to music education is further evidenced by the tremendous disparity between funding that is raised by parent councils at different schools within Ottawa: some school parent councils have raised tens of thousands of dollars to fund extracurricular activities (including music) for their children's school. In contrast, RSAS did not have a parent council when I began working with the school, let alone a budget to fund extracurricular activities such as music education; most RSAS parents are simply too busy trying to make ends meet and, in the case of the school's many recent immigrant families, trying to adjust to life in a new country. Even within Ottawa, a relatively affluent Canadian city, access to music education among children in the public education system is far from equal. Therefore, I felt grateful to be in a position to make music with the students at RSAS throughout the 2013–2014 school year.

Initially, I brought in a variety of instruments to the school, including shakers, rattles, and drums of various kinds, as well as a wide variety of musical instruments, including turntables for record scratching, iPads running music software applications, and an instrument known as the Reactable, a virtual modular synthesizer and digital sampler in the form of an interactive illuminated table: by placing and manipulating blocks on the Reactable surface, performers can control different parameters of prerecorded sounds in an intuitive way. We also used some comparatively low-tech musical instruments in the form of repurposed found objects, such as plastic buckets (which served as makeshift drums) and sonorous stones, which we rubbed and tapped together. I wanted to make it clear that everyone can make music, even if we don't have access to traditional musical instruments or traditional forms of musical instruction. Using these and other musical instruments (including our voices), we improvised together in the school's library every other week. I typically worked with two classes of similar age levels at a time (usually thirty and forty students) in each forty-five-minute session, working with each group one after the other, making music with all of the students at the school.

Early on in our collaboration, I learned that the students had developed a special connection to Mud Lake, an ecologically significant natural area adjacent to the school property. The principal and teachers at RSAS had integrated Mud Lake into multiple facets of the school's curriculum, cultivating the idea that RSAS students are the caretakers of Mud Lake. The students take this responsibility very seriously. Indeed, they have developed a detailed understanding of Mud Lake's ecology, history, and flora and fauna. Learning about Mud Lake from the students and teachers, I suggested that we could cocreate a musical performance that would take Mud Lake as its source of inspiration.

I introduced the students to R. Murray Schafer's concept of the "soundscape," the immersive sonic environment of a given place. I asked them to make note of all the sounds they heard on their weekly visits to Mud Lake: the "geophony" or earth sounds, such as wind in trees or raindrops on leaves and on the water; the "biophony" or animal sounds, including those of squirrels, beavers, frogs, and the more than two hundred bird species that have been spotted in the area; and the "anthrophony," or human sounds that animate the Mud Lake soundscape—those of birdwatchers and hikers, cars, and the nearby water filtration plant. I also asked them to take note of the ways in which the sounds of Mud Lake changed with the seasons as they found themselves walking through fallen leaves in the autumn and snow in the winter. Together, we researched the history of the area and imagined how the Mud Lake soundscape has changed over time. What did it sound like one hundred years ago, before there were cars? Or five hundred years ago, when the only human inhabitants of the area were the Algonquin First Nation? Or thirteen thousand years ago, when the glaciers retreated and the entire area was covered by the Champlain Sea?

Implicit in this process of sonic investigation and imagination was one of the pillars of critical pedagogy, namely the idea that students and teachers alike should become co-investigators of knowledge through critically engaged dialogue that leads to collaborative problem-solving in the service of a common learning objective. Our learning objective was to study the soundscape of Mud Lake and then work together to create a piece of music inspired by that soundscape, a piece that would feature both composed and improvised elements.

Through this collaborative process, we developed musical parts for all of the school's 160 students: the students in junior and senior kindergarten tapped stones together to create the sound of rain; the grades 1 and 2 students used ridged wooden frogs to create a chorus of frog sounds; the grades 3 and 4 students created bird sounds using bird calls and twelve turntables with LP records of bird sounds; the grades 5 and 6 students played drums. We also cowrote a part for a narrator, who would contextualize the sounds in the performance and help maintain the narrative flow of the piece.

Together, the school's entire student body and I premiered *Mud Lake Symphony* in the school's gymnasium in June 2014 for the families of RSAS students. Prior to the performance, we discussed how we would organize the concert space. Instead of setting up in a typical proscenium fashion, we decided to organize the students by grade such that they lined the perimeter of the gymnasium's walls: junior kindergarten and senior kindergarten students were positioned along one wall, grade 1 and 2 students along another, and so on. I was positioned in the center of the space, which allowed me to conduct each group and add sounds using the Reactable, waterphone, and frame drum. The chairs for the audience members were organized in concentric circles facing away from me and toward the students. The students felt that this spatial arrangement was an apt representation of Mud Lake: they thought of their parents as being in the middle of the lake and pictured themselves surrounding it.

The performance was enthusiastically received by the parents and school officials. Word of the project quickly spread, and we were invited to present the piece in a variety of settings. In the fall of 2014, we were invited to perform a version of *Mud Lake Symphony* to celebrate Global Dignity Day on October 15, 2014. A smaller group of roughly sixty students (grades 4 through 6) performed a condensed version of the piece as part of a national video conference that brought the students of RSAS into contact with fifteen hundred other schoolchildren from across Canada in a shared exploration and celebration of the concept of dignity. We were invited to perform the piece again at the Ottawa Carleton District School Board's "Spring into Leadership" conference in April 2015, this time with the addition of improviser and multi-instrumentalist William Parker, who happened to be in Ottawa that day for a performance with the Sonoluminescence Trio. In January 2016, we were invited to perform the piece at the Canadian New Music Network national forum, a biennial gathering of presenters and producers of new music from across Canada.

The *Mud Lake Symphony* project culminated in 2018 when we were invited to perform the piece at the National Arts Centre in Ottawa with the addition of the National Arts Centre Orchestra, one of the preeminent orchestras in Canada. The students in grades 5 and 6 and I developed a graphic score for the piece, which included parts for the members of the orchestra. Together, we performed the piece for four audiences of roughly two thousand people each in February 2018, showcasing the creativity of the students and the rich soundscape of Mud Lake.[27]

Each of these endeavors has built on the initial *Mud Lake Symphony* collaboration in generative ways, providing a broader range of learning experiences for the students of RSAS (and for me!) while affirming and expanding the sense of community engendered by the project. They also highlight the flexible nature of the piece—a function, at least in part, of the improvisatory nature of the piece and of the collaborative process. The highly flexible and adaptive nature of the *Mud Lake Symphony* project means that it can be used as a model for community-based collaborations in other contexts. Educators, students, and community members can adapt the piece—and the collaborative process that led to its creation—to the particularities of their own sonic, cultural, and educational environment, documenting the local soundscape and creating a community-affirming improvisatory performance inspired by it.

In 2013 and 2014, during roughly the same time frame that the students at RSAS and I were working on *Mud Lake Symphony*, I had the good fortune of collaborating with the artists at H'Art of Ottawa (now Being Studio), an organization that facilitates art making among adults with intellectual disabilities. The collaboration culminated in a multimedia performance titled *Turning the Page* that featured projected images of paintings by H'Art of Ottawa artists and a live improvised soundtrack that incorporated the sound of found objects, percussion instruments, and various electronic instruments.

From the beginning, the idea was to make the project as collaborative as possible. We didn't have any preconceived ideas about the form that our performance would ultimately take. Rather, we agreed that we would get together on a weekly basis to improvise with one another and see what emerged from the collaborative process. In a way, the *Turning the Page* performance emerged from a yearlong improvisation.

We decided to call the project *Turning the Page* because we felt as though we were turning the page, metaphorically speaking, on some of the ways in which art and music by persons with disabilities has been framed historically by dominant discourses surrounding contemporary cultural production, including many of those associated with so-called outsider art. All too often, outsider status is applied by people in positions of authority who claim to have discovered the work of marginalized artists and then benefit from the promotion, exhibition, performance, and publication of their work without much in the way of input from, or benefit to, the artists. This sort of exploitative practice is something we very much wanted to avoid.

Turning the Page was performed in Ottawa for a capacity audience at the National Arts Centre 4th Stage on April 30, 2014. At the outset of the performance, we enacted the idea of *Turning the Page* by handing out pieces of paper to all of the performers and audience members. The following words were printed on one side of the page along with an instruction for everyone to read the words out loud, preferably not in unison: "We are all artists. We are all musicians. We are turning the page on disability and the arts. We invite you to turn the page with us." At the bottom of the score are the words "Turn the Page." So the audience literally turned the page with the performers in a symbolic affirmation of our attempt to turn the page on received ideas about disability and the arts. On the back of each piece of paper was a list of instructions of ways that the piece of paper could be used to generate sound:

- Shake this piece of paper while holding it by one corner, varying the intensity of the shaking.
- Fold this piece of paper in half. Rub the two pieces of paper together, exploring patterned and unpatterned sounds.
- Tear this piece of paper into one continuous spiral.
- Fold this piece of paper in half. Place any of the three open edges between your lips and blow into the paper, causing it to act like a reed. Use long and short breath lengths, trying to vary the pitch of the resulting sounds.
- Holding the diagonal corners of this piece of paper, create percussive snapping sounds by quickly pulling the corners away from each other. Explore patterned and/or unpatterned sounds.

The performance began with all forty performers and all 180 audience members making music together in this way, putting all of us on the same page so to speak.

From there, we went on to explore the sound of cardboard boxes; percussion instruments, including drums, shakers, rattles, and gongs; and higher-tech instruments, including the Reactable. In *Turning the Page*, we used the Reactable to incorporate recordings of the artists talking about their creative practice and what art means to them. This was a low-stress way of incorporating everyone's voice into the piece; instead of having to experience the pressure of speaking in front of an audience, all the artists had to do was place blocks on the Reactable surface, which enabled them to weave their voices together in an affirmation of the dialogic spirit that animated the piece.

The Adaptive Use Musical Instrument, or AUMI, also occupied a central place in the performance. Initially conceived of by Pauline Oliveros, the Adaptive Use Musical Instrument is a free software application that turns any camera-equipped computer or iOS device into a flexible musical instrument in which movement triggers sound.[28] We used four AUMI-equipped iPads, which were positioned across the front of the stage. Several of the performers had a background in dance in addition to their background in the visual arts. The AUMI enabled us to incorporate a dance component into *Turning the Page* in a way that inverted the traditional relationship between dance and music: instead of the body responding to music, the movements of the improvising body caused the sounds, orchestrating the music.

Several unexpected things emerged from the yearlong collaborative process that led to the *Turning the Page* performance. For example, an Ottawa artist-run center called Gallery 101 expressed interest in the project and ended up mounting a major retrospective of works on paper by H'Art artists. Also titled *Turning the Page*, the exhibition was on display for two months prior to the performance. Something else to have emerged from the collaborative process was a documentary film about the project. An Ottawa-based filmmaker named Andrew Hall, who has a long-standing relationship with H'Art of Ottawa, filmed virtually every rehearsal as well as the exhibition at Gallery 101, the *Turning the Page* performance, and interviews with all of the participants. The video was premiered in November 2014 at the Power of the Arts National Forum in Ottawa and is available online.[29]

Jessie Huggett, an artist, dancer, and disability rights activist with Down syndrome who was involved in *Turning the Page*, had this to say about the experience:

> Collaboration for me as an artist is really important because we are working with other people, other artists and it opens lots of opportunities and possibilities. We really got to be more open—a sense of openness and diversity for everyone—the artists of H'Art Studio, the NAC staff, Gallery 101 and the people in our community. It's important to have openness because when we share our art, we share who we are as people. People in the community get to know the artists and they discover what we as artists have to offer the world.[30]

The kind of openness that Jessie Huggett describes was evident in a 2016 collaborative initiative with which WAAM was involved called Music Matters. In addition to WAAM, the Music Matters program was the result of a partnership between the Alzheimer's Society of Ottawa; Artswell, a nonprofit organization dedicated to using the arts to improve the quality of life and well-being of individuals living with the effects of age, illness, or injury; the Bruyère Continuing Care Centre in Ottawa; and the National Arts Centre. The project also included an Ottawa singer-songwriter named Julia Churchill who worked for Artswell.

Twice a week for eight weeks, Julia and I made music with a group of eight seniors living with Alzheimer's and other forms of dementia, as well as their caregivers who, in most cases, were their spouses. One thing that many members of the group had in common was a love for music. Several participants had extensive experience singing in choirs. One participant had even performed at the National Arts Centre some forty years earlier with a barbershop quartet. Other participants had little or no prior experience performing music, but nonetheless shared a passion for music. At each session, we would sing songs together and improvise with one another using a variety of percussion instruments. At one of our sessions, a participant named Felix, who was eighty-five at the time, said "I like to sing with my feet." He went on to explain that he preferred dancing to singing. So we incorporated the Adaptive Use Musical Instrument into our biweekly gatherings in such a way that, as Felix danced, the AUMI would translate his movements into sound. AUMI provided a gateway into the music, enabling him to participate in a manner that was fun and enjoyable for him.

Part of the intention behind the Music Matters program was to provide an opportunity for all of the participants to have a new musical experience that would be shared by both those with dementia and their caregivers. Through an eight-week-long process of musical improvisation, exploration, and dialogue, we cocreated an original piece that combined music, poetry, and dance, performing the results of our collaboration at the National Arts Centre on May 1, 2016. The performance included some favorite songs of the participants, including "Accentuate the Positive" and "Bye Bye Blackbird," as well as a new song that we cowrote using memories that the participants had shared with the group as the basis for the lyrics. The performance also included two original poems by members of the group, one that celebrated the power and beauty of music, and another titled "Lost for Words," that one of the participants who had recently turned ninety wrote about the age-related cognitive changes that she was experiencing. As in *Turning the Page*, we used the Reactable to incorporate the voices of the participants in the performance, layering audio recordings that we had made in the weeks leading up to the performance of participants sharing their memories with us.

The performance also included two renditions of "You Are My Sunshine," a favorite melody of several participants. In addition to singing it as a group, we performed a deconstructed version of the piece in which I played the melody on the vibraphone with my right hand while providing improvised drum set accompaniment with my left hand and feet. Upon successive repetitions of the melody, I left out an increasing number of notes while Julia Churchill removed parts of my drum set one piece at a time, thereby reflecting, both musically and performatively, some of the cognitive changes that the participants had experienced. As Julia removed the drum set components, she gave them to the participants, who began improvising on them with sticks and mallets. This gesture was intended to be a symbolic affirmation of the idea that as we age and begin to experience gaps in our memory, others around us—our loved ones and those in our community—are able to help fill in those gaps for and with us.

Angela Parić, a doctoral candidate in the Health Sciences Department at Carleton University, studied the health impacts of the Music Matters program, finding that care recipients' levels of enjoyment and willingness to initiate music making significantly increased throughout the program.[31] In general, care recipients were "more relaxed, content, and cognitively engaged" during and after Music Matters sessions than they were at the outset.[32] "It makes me happy. It makes me very happy," said one participant.[33] Another said, "It means a fair bit, because we enjoy music and we enjoy the people here. We're all probably more or less in the same boat."[34] A third participant agreed: "Numero uno. Number 1. That's all I can say. [The group] means a lot to me. It means much. . . . Music is always up for me, always. I love music and of course I love dancing too."[35] In addition, several participants indicated that the experience had a positive impact on their cognitive health. One participant said, "It keeps my brain moving. It makes me think."[36] Another stated, "Singing is a very healing thing at any time. And it's also fun."[37]

The Music Matters project, much like *Mud Lake Symphony* and *Turning the Page*, highlighted the capacity of musical improvisation to bring people together in an inclusive way, to promote health and well-being, and to foster a sense of community.

Musical Improvisation at Land's End / Coin-du-Banc en folie

In August 2016, IICSI launched the inaugural version of a weeklong bilingual (French and English) summer musical improvisation camp, Musical Improvisation at Land's End (MILE) / Coin-du-Banc en folie, in the Gaspésie region of Quebec.[38] Organized by Ajay Heble and Alain Chalifour, this community-engaged research-creation initiative seeks to develop innovative strategies to put musicians with varying levels of improvisation experience in direct and meaningful contact with professional improvisers, and to engage young musicians and nonmusicians alike in hands-on workshops. The inaugural edition of the camp featured improviser-mentors clarinetist François Houle (British Columbia), vocalist Kathy Kennedy (Quebec), and percussionist Jesse Stewart (Ontario). The workshops focused on nurturing and developing musical improvisation as a vital model of arts-based community-making. The objectives were to connect members of diverse communities with improvisatory experiences and to foster collaboration and understanding between people from diverse urban and rural backgrounds. We wanted to facilitate participants' creativity and foster a sense of confidence in themselves as musicians, and as members of a community. The camp built on networks and partnerships with La Société historique de Coin-du-Banc / Corner of the Beach Historical Society, a nonprofit organization that runs a historical museum on the site of the recently deconsecrated St. Luke's Anglican Church, and the Festival Musique du Bout du Monde, a distinctive and well-established community-based world music festival in the town of Gaspé. Many community members saw the camp initiative as vital work for the region, especially given the significant problem of youth exodus in the Gaspésie region, a problem noted by the Carrefour Jeunesse Emploi MRC Côte-de-Gaspé.[39] The idea of a summer improvisation camp in the region was also in keeping with IICSI's mandate to create positive social change through the confluence of improvisational arts, scholarship, collaboration, and education. The inaugural version of MILE camp brought together musicians of different ages and levels of expertise: internationally acclaimed professional musicians played side by side with music students and with members of the community. The camp provided an inclusive and supportive environment for musical exploration incorporating traditional instruments, found objects, and cutting-edge interactive technologies. Together, participants explored new and innovative approaches to creating improvised music, testing the inner traditions and the outer limits of the music: the group created, arranged, rehearsed, performed, improvised, and learned together. Throughout the week, participants took part in workshops on musical improvisation, deep listening, site-specific improvisation, sonic experimentation, collaborating across genres, graphic scores, assistive/adaptive use technologies, choral improvisation, and conducted improvisation. Participants also had the opportunity to perform onstage in public settings, including a performance at the Festival Musique du Bout du Monde.

Data was gathered through participant observation; open-ended, semistructured entrance interviews with the seven participants and three artist facilitators, as well as with attendees and community members; exit interviews with the participants and artist facilitators; and video documentation of workshops, lecture-demonstrations, and performances. This data gathering was supplemented by oral histories about the region gathered through interviews with members of the local community. All interviews included open-ended questions. These questions addressed the evaluative features of the workshop and concert settings, such as strengths and weaknesses, benefits, and reactions, as well as analytical factors, including pedagogical goals, modes of preparation, and tools for teaching improvisation.

During the entrance interviews, participants and artist facilitators were asked about their past experience with improvised music and their hopes and expectations for the camp. Community members were asked to comment on what the summer camp project might mean for them and for the region. During exit interviews, participants and artist facilitators were asked to describe the impact the camp has had for them: "What will you take away from your week with us in Coin-du-Banc? What are the main stories you will be remembering, and the key lessons you have learned?" ("Quel sont les histoires dont vous allez vous souvenir, et les lessons que vous avez appris?") They were also asked whether the camp confirmed or challenged any of the expectations they might have had when they began ("Quelles étaient vos attentes avant d'arriver au camp?"), and whether their experience with the summer camp had in any way changed their assumptions about improvisation ("Comment est-ce que le camp a répondu (ou non) à vos attentes?").

Making use of distinctive spaces and venues, including one of the Gaspésie's most pristine beaches, a deconsecrated church, a geodesic dome installed on the beach specifically for the camp, an auberge known for its cuisine and its hospitality, and a charming and spacious guest house, the camp was designed to take advantage of the region's many attractions, especially its stunning natural beauty. The Gaspé coast has been listed by *National Geographic* as one of the top twenty tourist destinations in the entire world (and the only one in Canada). Nestled in the most easterly tip of the region appropriately known as the Land's End, and minutes away from the famous Rocher Percé, the coastal village of Coin-du-Banc, where the camp was located, offered an inspirational natural setting for a summer camp devoted to musical improvisation. Our contention was that where the land ends, imagination begins.

Comments made about the setting capture something of the magic of off-the-beaten-track locations. In his exit interview, François Houle remarked about the importance, indeed the vitality, of having marginalized and experimental artistic practices, and festivals that feature these practices, "popping up in the oddest of places" and "in an environment where nobody thought it could be done." "The name of the game," as author Marian Salzman writes in an article in the *Huffington Post*, "is placemaking—building the unique identity and appeal of a location. It's about the transformation of a nowhere place that's off the beaten track, or an anywhere place that's superficially like thousands of others, into a somewhere—a distinctive place with its own attractive personality. The stakes can be high, but the payoff can make it well worth the price."[40] I (Ajay) have certainly been drawn to the idea of bringing experimental and innovative forms of music making to remote locations, to settings outside metropolitan centers, to places where you wouldn't expect to hear such music. Bringing a musical improvisation camp to the remote coastal village of Coin-du-Banc in the Gaspésie region of Quebec, then, is in many ways consistent with the work (described elsewhere in this book) that I have done with the Guelph Jazz Festival. It's about engaging in a process of placemaking, and indeed of arts-based community-making, that seeks to highlight, animate, and celebrate "a distinctive place with its own attractive personality." Other festivals of improvised and experimental musics that have engaged in a similar process of place-making in smaller communities include the Electric Eclectics Festival in Meaford, Ontario and Le festival international de musique actuelle in Victoriaville, Quebec.

The interviews we conducted for the MILE camp make it clear that the participants benefited from the opportunity to learn improvisation from professional improvising musicians, developing musicianship, skills, and confidence by taking musical risks in a supportive and inclusive environment. One of the significant defining principles that Lee Higgins associates with practitioners of community music is that they "seek to foster confidence in participants' creativity."[41] Workshops throughout the week built the confidence of participants as performers. Some participants had lived experience with anxiety, attention deficit disorder, and autism spectrum disorder. Participants differed greatly in terms of stage experience, and several experienced stage fright before their first live performance. However, by the end of the week, all participants demonstrated an increase in confidence in themselves as performers and were able to participate in a final performance (a performance that François Houle described as "one of my highlights of playing this year") that drew on improvisational skills developed throughout the course of the camp.

The driftwood xylophone that the participants constructed as a group, as well as the AUMI, were especially helpful in extending an inclusive invitation to all performers to participate, as was the general emphasis on collaboration and experimentation over individual virtuosity.

Particularly noteworthy, and for both of us a key breakthrough moment, was the fact that one of the participants, Olivia, who spoke to us about her anxiety, decided, somewhat unexpectedly, to perform during the final public concert at the museum. Throughout the week, she seemed to be apart from the rest of the group. When invited to join in collaborative music-making activities, she would often decline, preferring for the most part to remain on the sidelines watching and listening. She had indicated to us that she would not be performing with the group at the final concert, as she would find it too anxiety-inducing. Olivia also told us that she had a background in ballet, and although the thought of performing musically was very stressful to her, dancing tended to put her at ease. Upon hearing this, we installed several iPads running the AUMI software inside the geodesic dome that we had set up on the beach. We invited her to spend some time in the space by herself, moving and dancing as she saw fit, allowing the AUMI to translate her movements into sound. Her experiences with the AUMI seemed to boost her confidence because at the last minute she decided to join the final concert after all. Drawing on her dance background, she used the AUMI to translate her improvised movements into sound, which added considerably to the performance both musically and visually. During her exit interview, she too spoke about a sense of confidence and an ability to "go with the flow" that improvisation had enabled. Reflecting on the camp as a "once in a lifetime" experience, Olivia explained, "I am doing things now I never dreamed I would."

Another key feature of the camp that contributed to the sense of confidence noted by many of the participants was the emphasis on dialogic pedagogy—an issue we have discussed in some detail in our chapter on co-learning. Most of the camp participants remarked upon this feature of the camp. For example, Theo, who at fifteen years of age was the camp's youngest participant, spoke about the camp's familial ambiance, while Ian Gibbons was more forthright in explaining that participants felt as though they were treated as colleagues: "We didn't really feel like students," he explained. The instructors, too, made the point that they didn't see themselves as "teachers" in the traditional or conventional sense, emphasizing instead their role as facilitators and participants. As we have already noted, one of central tenets of critical pedagogy is the idea that students must be active agents in their own process of learning, and that when it comes to music education, improvisation provides a unique opportunity to examine and transform conventional relationships between teachers and students, as well as relationships played out on the bandstand, and within the wider communities in which we live, work, and learn. In this context, it's worth pointing out, as Kathy Kennedy did, that participants during the camp consistently looked out for one another, that there was a "level of trust where people can thrive." This sense of trust played a key role in enabling participants to collaborate across multiple forms of difference. One camp participant, who is an accomplished and classically trained McGill University music student, admitted during his exit interview that he had "never been in such a diverse group of musicians." This may seem an odd statement for someone studying at a university in a city as culturally rich and diverse as Montreal, but what it perhaps suggests is that such opportunities for music making across boundaries of age, class, language, ethnicity, race, and ability remain all too rare, which makes community-oriented learning initiatives like the MILE camp all the more important.

If, as Lee Higgins contends, community music involves a recognition "that participants' social and personal growths are as important as their musical growth,"[42] then perhaps the impact that community-oriented improvisational pedagogical initiatives such as Musical Improvisation at Land's End / Coin-du-Banc en folie can have on participants can be summed up in these words from camp participant Ian: "I came for the music, but I ended up being better developed as a person."

Partnering for Change:
Learning outwards from Musical Improvisation

The case studies we've considered in this chapter open up important questions about what creative partnerships might teach us about collaboration across sectors, genres, and abilities; about the ways in which people and organizations learn, grow, and change through partnerships; and about the methodologies that can come into play when musicians, artists, community members, and academics come together in community-based improvisation pedagogies. We learned a great deal from our involvement in the projects described here, growing as students, teachers, and scholars of improvisation. And while our chapter certainly isn't meant to be read as an educational instruction manual, we offer this summary of some of the core lessons that we have learned in an effort to move outward from the specific case studies under consideration:

1. *Diversifying our sonic and epistemic palettes.* Saxophonist Matana Roberts—an artist who participated in the earliest iteration of the Play Who You Are workshops in Guelph and in Montreal—has coined the phrase "panoramic soundquilting" to describe her own method of music making: her attraction "to a certain sort of collagist aesthetic," to "what happens when all these sounds cross that are not necessarily completely related to each other. Then you listen back to them and it creates this whole other sonic palette."[43] The kind of sound-crossing and boundary-shattering music that Roberts describes as a core part of the process of expanding our sonic palette seems an apt way for us to think about what has so clearly become a salient feature of the partner-based improvised musical collaborations we consider in this chapter, namely the importance of broadening and diversifying our base of valued knowledges. Such attention to diversity, as we've tried to suggest throughout this book, is critical in our present moment. Think again of Cecil Foster's claim, "Life is messy: it is about different and diverse people having no bigger challenge than to get along together . . . an achievement for which there is no guarantee."[44] And recall, too, Ien Ang's contention, "One of the most urgent predicaments of our time can be described in deceptively simple terms: how are we to live together in this new century?"[45] As the instances we describe in this chapter make clear, improvisation has a special capacity to negotiate various types of difference. Just as the staging and sounding of diversity that festivals of improvised music can enable in their communities, so too can community-based pedagogies of improvisation play a role in advancing the struggle for a more inclusive repertoire of valued knowledges.

2. *What partnership means for us.* From the beginning, we've been concerned in our work on improvisational practices and pedagogy to reach beyond the academy, beyond the classroom, into other communities, and to redefine what counts as "research." Instead of "research on," we have sought through our partnerships to adopt a model of "research with" a diverse range of participants. We are committed to looking beyond the conventional classroom to find ways to democratize our research outputs. In working with

partners to integrate improvisational arts-based activity into social and educational programs for various aggrieved, marginalized, and at-risk communities in cities across Canada, one of the things we've learned is what partnership really means: for us, it has meant that we need to see collaboration and consultation as core first principles of our method. This point is worth stressing: projects that require the engagement of multiple academic and community partners require significant effort, skill, and code-switching to be managed successfully. "Success," in this context, involves the capacity to work closely with our partners to design, implement, disseminate, and evaluate research activities and to engage in cross-sector decision-making and a cocreative process of knowledge exchange, while always remaining responsive to the needs of the communities with which we're partnering. The development of joint agendas helps to ensure that there is a clear fit between what the academic researchers and university partners can offer (in terms of research needs and priorities, and availability of resources) and what community partners need or expect. At issue here is also the fact that large-scale, multisector collaborations necessitate a willingness to adapt to the needs of the moment. In other words, we can learn a great deal from improvisation itself as a model for partnership-building.

3. *Rethinking expertise and putting pressure on conventional disciplinary allegiances.* In designing projects and conducting research on community-based improvisation pedagogies, we cannot assume to know where the right answers (or even the right questions) might come from. Instead, our own learning process must be improvisatory in nature as we continually listen and adapt in a spirit of ongoing dialogic and collaborative inquiry. In challenging received assumptions about the nature of expertise, we also seek to challenge assumptions about where knowledge resides, and about methodologies surrounding academic research. Indeed, we want to question—and broaden—the understanding of what counts as academic research.

Part of what's at stake, then, is the need to rethink the very places where we look for knowledge. In our case, this has meant listening to—and learning from—other scholars and creative practitioners, as well as persons with disabilities, young people, older people, and marginalized and historically aggrieved communities. In short, one of the key lessons we've learned from our research is that we shouldn't go into communities with assumptions about how to make things better; rather, our efforts should be focused on engaging with communities to understand the issues at play and the terms of engagement. Again, it's vital that we go beyond using community partners as sources of data, as objects of study. How can we involve our partners meaningfully in cocreation and co-research, that is, in the design, implementation, and evaluation of our research and pedagogy? This is the question we must continue to ask.

4. *Legacy and sustainability.* As educators who engage with community partners and bring our work into broader communities of interest and involvement, we must attend to the long-term implications of this work. What will happen when we leave? What will happen when the resources we're able to mobilize for improvisational workshops in the community are no longer available? How might we work with our partners to ensure ongoing forms of institutional support so that there might be a replication of the pedagogical efforts our partnered initiatives have set in motion? How might we find ways to extend the life of our collaborative work?

   These questions can be particularly important for populations who have experienced some form of loss. A key lesson learned for us has been that these questions need to be considered during the planning process. We need to work with our partners to ensure that this kind of goal-setting and longer-term thinking is factored into the design of our pedagogy and research. It's also, in this context, useful to think about the legacy of our work, how others might take it up in their own communities. To that end, one of the outcomes of some of the activities described in this chapter has been a tool kit of techniques for teaching improvisation that was developed by Ellen Waterman and Rob Jackson (at the time a University of Guelph undergraduate student intern), with input from many ICASP/IICSI researchers. The tool kit, which includes downloadable activities and practical guides for leading improvisation workshops, is available for free online for educators, community organizations, and anyone else who is interested.[46]

5. *Not just the pedagogy of improvisation but also improvisational pedagogies.* The initiatives and activities we've described in this chapter have taught us that, in designing and implementing community-based music pedagogies of improvisation, we need to be open and responsive to the needs, desires, and competencies of the people

with whom we are collaborating. Rather than walking into communities with a fixed plan of action, with fully scripted plans for pedagogical implementation, there will be situations where we will need to adapt, to be flexible, to change our plans. In short, effective pedagogies of improvisation demand improvisational pedagogies. This means that we that we must be able to respond in real time and to adjust (and possibly reinvent) our methods as situations demand.

6. *"A Whole World of Possibilities."* Giving the impossible a chance: in the *Stories of Impact* film about Katy we referenced earlier in our discussion about the Play Who You Are partnership with KidsAbility, Katy's mother, Barbara, talks about how improvisation has opened up "a whole world of possibilities" for her daughter. This puts us in mind of Ellen Waterman's response to the panel discussion with William Parker, quoted at the outset of this chapter, about how improvisation can function as a force that's active in the world. But despite her appreciation of the possibilities, Barbara is also forthright in reminding us that "Katy's world is full of limitations." Her comment about limitations is important. It reminds us that, for all its potential as an agent of social change, improvisation won't always triumph over adversity. What we've learned from our ten years of research with the Play Who You Are initiative, as indeed with all of the projects we've described in this chapter, is the importance of cultivating resources for hope, of nourishing opportunities for change, of giving the seemingly impossible a chance, even as our projects take us into spaces and places where there will continue to be complex negotiations, contradictions, compromises, challenges, and limitations. That sense of hope and change, that "world of possibilities" is often manifest not necessarily in large-scale or spectacular transformations, but rather in what Elizabeth Jackson has referred to as "small, fleeting moments: unpin-downable interactions, flashes of eye contact, the smile on [the] face of a very unexpressive child."[47] Another musician with a history of involvement as a workshop facilitator with the Play Who You Are project and other improvisation-based initiatives, drummer and scholar Rob Wallace, has put it this way: "If we work together with a common goal, in this case, the performance at the Jazz Festival, we can grow and change and get better even in the face of physical and mental challenges that conventional wisdom says are fixed and unsurmountable."[48] Indeed, as Daniel Fischlin has written, "Improvi-

sation is a constant reminder that it is possible to hope—and to do so in response to conditions that seek to limit human possibility and creativity."[49]

Such resources for hope are in direct contrast to the culture of acquiescence or nonparticipation that asks us to resign ourselves to the way things are because (or so we are too often told), no other future is possible. Improvisation, we believe, can teach us otherwise. It can encourage us to enact the very possibilities we envision. Our success in solving some of the most crucial problems we're facing, now and in the future, may well depend on our capacity to develop new models of thought and action, on our ability to break out of conventional, recurrent solution-patterns—in short, on our ability to improvise and to give the impossible a chance.

Coda

Performance as Pedagogy

"The musical situation that I found myself eager to describe," writes author and musician David Grubbs in the afterword to his book-length prose poem *Now that the Audience is Assembled,* "is a concert of experimental or improvised music."[1] While such a description, Grubbs confesses, may not appear to tell us much, this "initially baggy subject" for his poem, as it turns out,

> became the opportunity to write about solo performance, free improvisation, text scores, instrument building, time killing, masochism, performer psychology, audience behavior, audience and performer bad behavior, the all-night concert, waking up in the midst of a concert, the deskilling and reskilling of conventionally trained musicians, the curious and occasionally vestigial role of the composer in experimental music, a lifetime of fraught relations with one's first instrument, and more.[2]

And more, indeed. Grubbs's compact but expansive experimental poem reveals the extent to which the description of an artistic practice or endeavour—in this case, a fictional night-long live performance of improvised music—can, borrowing again from the definition of pedagogy we've cited from Henry Giroux, illuminate "the complicated processes by which knowledge is produced, skills are learned meaningfully, identities are shaped, desires are mobilized, and critical dialogue becomes a central form of public interaction."[3] Knowledge, identities, skills, desires, and dialogue, after all, are at the heart of the public sets

124

of interactions described when the audience is assembled for the performance in Grubbs's poem; all are mobilized in and through the practice of musical improvisation. And the author's comments in his Afterword about the rippling out from his "initially baggy subject" offer a useful way for us to reflect on arguments we've been making throughout this book about the individual, collaborative, institutional, and community-oriented dimensions of musical improvisation as interrelated sites of pedagogical practice.

In *Humanism and Democratic Criticism,* Edward Said states that pedagogy necessarily "involves widening circles of awareness, each of which is distinct analytically while being connected to the others by virtue of worldly reality."[4] For Said, the work that humanities teachers and scholars do must "move beyond and inhabit more than just the original privacy of the writer or the relatively private space of the classroom."[5] "Yes," he says, "we need to keep coming back to the words and structures in the books we read, but, just as these words were themselves taken by the poet from the world and evoked from out of silence in the forceful ways without which no creation is possible, readers must also extend their readings out into the various worlds each of us resides in."[6] Said isn't explicitly writing here (as he has elsewhere) about music, but we'd like to extend his argument about reading literature and make a similar claim about listening to and learning from music. Said's insistence on the necessity of education's involvement with widening circles of awareness, with extended frameworks of analysis and interpretation, is, it seems to us, very much in keeping with Grubbs's notion, expressed in and through his poem, of improvised musical performance as "real-time, public research."[7] And this notion of "real-time, public research" resonates with George Lewis's suggestion that free improvisation has "blurred the boundaries between improvisation as performance, as critical musical inquiry, and as political and social activism, all in the course of researching new sounds and modes of communication."[8] Add to this our understanding and assessment of the ways in which the improvisational practices and pedagogies of musicians and community groups can model—and enact—new forms of community-making, critical thinking, and social practice, and we are reminded once again of bell hooks's central claim that teaching and learning are going on all around us.

The "widening circles of awareness" we've sought to employ in the very structure of our book, the movement outward from autodidactic models of learning through processes associated with co-learning and mentorship to discussions of the learning that takes place within alternative pedagogical institutions, more formal academic contexts, and community-oriented frameworks, make it clear that we need to rethink the places where we look for knowledge: education takes place not only within the familiar walls of the academic classroom, but also in unstressed, unconventional, or unexpected spaces and places. Grubbs's poem, for instance, reminds us of something we might tend to overlook: the act of improvisational musical performance itself offers an educational experience, as well as a musical and social one. Riffing on Grubbs's notion of "real time, public research," we'd like to explore what it might mean to think about performance as "real time, public" pedagogy. Clearly, as we've already suggested in various ways throughout the book, important learning takes place, both for the audience and for the performers, in an improvised musical performance. Think of the learning that takes place when audience members have an opportunity to watch improvising artists perform (recall, for example, our earlier description of the impact of watching percussionist Gerry Hemingway perform live for the first time). To our discussions of the pedagogy that is enacted through individual, collaborative, institutional, and community-oriented dimensions of musical improvisation, we must, then, remember to add the bandstand, and to consider real time public performance itself as a critical pedagogical site.

Most of the literature on performance and/as pedagogy tends to think of the experience of teaching as a performative act. But what does it mean to flip the script and instead to consider the act and experience of performance itself as a kind of pedagogy? In his essay "Pedagogy on the Move: New Intersections in (Between) the Educative and the Performative," sociologist Greg Dimitriadis grapples with this question as he describes the process through which he "came to see popular culture (such as hip hop) as an alternative curriculum and community-based organizations . . . as alternative learning settings."[9] Just as we have argued that the pedagogy of musical improvisation needs to be understood as part of a complex and ongoing process, one that operates through a wide variety of interconnected individual self-learning activities and experiences, "alternative learning settings," and broader collaborative and institutional practices, Dimitriadis suggests that "the performative decenters our taken-for-granted assumptions about pedagogy—where it happens and with what texts."[10] Like us, Dimitriadis is prompted to "look for education in unsuspecting places."[11]

To engage in such looking (and, given our focus on musical improvisation, we would add such sounding) is not only to reinvigorate our understanding of *where* (and under what conditions) we learn, but also to open up questions about *how, what,* and *why* we learn. Returning to Grubbs's poem, we find that its attention to, and emphasis on, the complex role played by the audience (described here as "alternately contemplative, participatory, disputatious, and asleep")[12] reminds us of the critical point that the knowledge being negotiated during a real-time musical performance is part of an ongoing dialogue that involves listeners and performing artists alike, and that the performance constitutes an act in which teaching and learning are going on simultaneously.

How, then, do we learn? We learn, as Freire's critical, problem-posing model of pedagogy might suggest, by being part of the dialogue, whether we are musical performers, or we are listeners who, as Grubbs's fictional all-night performance makes clear, can choose their own pathways through the music. It's important to note that "the habit of dialogue," as our friend and colleague George Lipsitz has pointed out, isn't solely the property of "traditional intellectuals who write books and articles."[13] Rather, it needs to be understood as "an essential way of understanding the world for all historical actors."[14] Throughout this book, we have sought to take our cue from Lipsitz when, as we've cited earlier, he tells us that we, as "'traditional intellectuals' in institutions of higher learning" must "develop forms of academic criticism capable of comprehending the theorizing being done at the grassroots level by artists and their audiences, of building bridges between different kinds of theory."[15] Grubbs's book, it seems to us, is engaged precisely in such bridge-building: it blurs any easy distinctions we might want to make between theory and practice, or between music and poetry. And it's an apt example of a project that reveals a kind of grassroots theorizing, highlighting perspectives from both performers and their audiences.

Trombonist David Dove, in describing the music-making he has done over the years at Nameless Sound, an organization he founded in Houston, Texas that organizes improvisation-based workshops and performances in a range of community settings (such as schools, women's shelters, housing projects), makes a related point when he explains that the practice of music-making in itself "would reveal new understandings of its applications and its possibilities. The *music,*" Dove maintains, "is the pedagogy."[16] Another trombonist, Scott Thomson, similarly stresses the pedagogical dimensions of the music and the "scene" surrounding the music: "For musicians who wish to improvise (of any age, trained in any style of music, at any level of technical proficiency), the network of performances within a scene presents a fluid environment for their improvisatory education."[17]

What do we learn through this fluid environment, this network of performances that constitute our improvisatory education? We learn to listen, certainly. More suggestively, we learn how to cultivate purposeful resources for listening, how, that is, to be curious, attentive, and (to invoke Pauline Oliveros once again) deep listeners. We learn also how to negotiate various kinds of differences, how to make do with the situations in which we find ourselves, with the materials that are available to us. But we also learn that performances of improvised music are not neutral expressions in the circulation of meaning; rather, they are themselves complex pedagogical acts that can teach us different ways of sounding, and being, in the world, ways of interacting with others that are based on cooperation, collaboration, and mutual respect.

This brings us to *why* we learn? If we learn in an effort to give the impossible a chance, to break out of conventional, recurrent solution-patterns, then how might such chance-giving, such breaking-out, be animated by and enacted through efforts to jam the classroom—indeed, the many classrooms—where musical improvisation takes place, both inside and out of conventional educational settings, both on the bandstand and off?

There's a memory that both of us share of a performance of improvised music that seems pertinent to the questions we are raising here. Flashback to the Guelph Jazz Festival in 1997. The audience is assembled, and Pauline Oliveros has taken the stage in the sanctuary of a historic church. She is about to begin her solo accordion recital. Just at the moment that she begins to play, we hear the first rumble of distant thunder. As she continues to play, the thunder grows louder and louder until booming shock waves reverberate throughout the church, and streaks of lightning flash against the stain-glass windows. There's an incredible intensity to this storm, and it's suddenly dark and ominous-looking both outside and in the sanctuary of the church. But Oliveros doesn't seem daunted. She reacts to the frenzy of the storm not by trying to match its intensity, but rather by listening, and by improvising on her accordion, slowly and carefully. Then an amazing thing happens. About an hour or so after she begins performing, Oliveros winds down to a close. And just as she plays her final meandering notes, the storm, as if on cue, abruptly stops. The storm and the performance both stop at the same time. This is not like anything we've seen or heard before. It's an extraordinary experience. Is this perhaps what giving the impossible a chance looks and sounds like? Is this what it means to break away from recurrent solution-patterns?

We're tempted to look back on that performance as a one-of-a-kind experience, but when we've described it to others, we've been told other amazing stories about Pauline's performances, stories that exemplify her practice of, and her commitment to, Deep Listening: "listening," as she has described and defined the practice, "in every possible way to every thing possible to hear no matter what you are doing. Such intense listening includes the sounds of daily life, of nature, of one's own thoughts as well as musical sounds."[18] There's one story, for example, about a time when she was performing at an outdoor concert with intensely heavy traffic noise that might have threatened to drown out the music. But when Pauline began to play, we were told, all the sounds from the traffic suddenly seemed to merge with the music, all the sounds (even those that might have initially seemed distracting) became an integral part of the performance. The setting, in short, was transformed.[19] As with the concert we've described from Guelph, this story about Pauline, too, shows what can happen when we listen deeply, whether as performers or as audiences of improvised music: this ability to make do with the situations (and the environments) in which we find ourselves, to change our perception of a given situation and perhaps that of those around us (sometimes even in what might seem to be the most distracting or discouraging circumstances), is the hallmark of a good deep listener.

Having performed with Pauline Oliveros on numerous occasions since witnessing her remarkable duet with the thunderstorm, I (Jesse) have witnessed, and shared in, several similarly remarkable experiences of Deep Listening, experiences that left a lasting impression on me as profound musical and learning experiences. For example, in 2013, I had the great honour of performing with Pauline and Stuart Dempster—two of the founding members of the Deep Listening Band—along with saxophonist Jonas Braasch, percussionist Johannes Welsch, and vocalist Ione in a performance that marked the 25th anniversary of the Deep Listening Band's debut recording, titled simply *Deep Listening*. *Deep Listening* is a landmark work in the history of experimental music and improvised music. It is also one of my favourite recordings. Needless to say, I was thrilled to have been asked to participate in this anniversary concert and recording session.

The original *Deep Listening* recording is notable for many reasons, not the least of which is the fact that it was recorded in the Fort Worden cistern (which is now known as the Dan Harpole Cistern), a two-million gallon underground chamber that was emptied in the 1950s, creating a cavernous space with a remarkable reverberation time of 45 seconds.

For the 25th anniversary concert in Ottawa, Jonas Braasch recreated the acoustics of the cistern through digital means, adding 45 seconds of reverb to every sound that we played.[20] The performance was an exercise in restraint and disciplined Deep Listening because every sound that we contributed continued to reverberate for 45 seconds after the initial improvisatory impulse. So we all had to choose our sounds, and the timing of our sounds, wisely. Over the course of the hour-long concert, I probably only added a few dozen sound events to the mix because of the intense reverb and the density of the sound. Silence and attentive listening to the totality of the group sound were of paramount importance.

For me, the most extraordinary aspect of the performance was its conclusion and its aftermath. When the five us seemed to collectively sense that we had reached the end of the performance, we stopped sounding on our respective instruments and listened together as the culmination of our combined soundings gradually receded into silence. As I listened to that sonic decay, I had a very interesting experience: there came a point where I was no longer certain if I was still actually hearing the reverberation of our music, or if I was just remembering the sound, hearing it in my imagination. I think other people in attendance may have had a similar experience to mine because a remarkable thing happened after the music had faded: the audience was silent. Not just for a few seconds. For 1 minute and 25 seconds. No one applauded. No one coughed. No one whispered. No one shifted in their seats. We all just sat there, being together, listening in silence, reflecting on the experience that we had just shared. That extended silence was another one of the most powerful listening experiences of my life. It was certainly one of the most profound examples of Deep Listening that I have ever experienced.

Returning now to Pauline's memorable Guelph performance in 1997, I (Ajay) recall Pauline saying to me that she felt as if she had been improvising with God as her musical partner that night. This was perhaps her way of stressing that even when an artist is performing improvised music in a solo context, he or she is never really alone, her way of pointing to the widening circles of awareness at play in improvised music. As we reflect back on that evening, and on our experiences with Pauline Oliveros more generally, what seems particularly striking to us is how Pauline's theory of Deep Listening was embodied in the practice, and how we were witness not only to real-time musical decision-making and risk-taking, but also to a generous sense of what it means to engage in collaborative improvisation, to hear what the other has to play, even when one is performing solo. That concert taught us that one of the great benefits of being part of a performance of improvised music is to be found in the experience, and perhaps also the pleasure, of meditating on the challenges of risk and contingency, on the ways in which our listening strategies can shake us out of our ingrained habits of response and judgement. This is so not only for the musician(s) on stage, but also for those of us taking in the performance as audience members.

Just by being there, in other words, we learned that night how the particularities associated with performance situations can transform our understanding, our attention, our habits of response. And this, we would suggest, is a core part of *why* we learn to improvise: to unsettle fixity, to liberate ourselves from having to respond to life situations with a pre-digested point of view, to reinvigorate our capacity to hear and to see the world anew. In the current social moment, we suggest, this kind of learning—the "perspective-jarring turnabout" that can happen when we jam the classroom—takes on new urgency. More than ever, we need to subject our relationship to the world(s) around us to careful, ongoing, and rigorous scrutiny. More than ever, we need to learn how to listen deeply, curiously, critically. We need to learn how to collaborate and to solve problems, collectively.

The extended frameworks of analysis and interpretation that, for us, were so cogently and profoundly embodied in Pauline's performance that evening are somewhat akin to David Grubbs's Afterword to his prose poem, his discussion of the ripple effects generated from his initial impetus to describe "a concert of experimental or improvised music."[21] There is, as the rippling out in Grubbs's poem makes clear, nothing easy or routine about essaying such a description. Meditating on such widening circles of awareness can, as both Grubbs's poem and our experience of Pauline's concert suggest, offer an apt reminder of the complex and varied ways in which teaching and learning are going on in the many classrooms of improvisation. Learning by doing. Learning by listening and watching. Learning by hearing what the other has to play. Learning in unsuspecting spaces and places. And, as we reflect back on Pauline's concert, we recognize the extent to which learning in a performance of improvised music can take place simply by *being there*, by being in the moment, by sharing an experience, and by listening deeply. We were *there* when Pauline improvised with the thunderstorm. It is to her memory, and to the learning she inspired, that we dedicate this book.

Notes

Preface

   1. Scherstuhl, "William Parker."

   2. It's worth remarking that William Parker has been consistent in his messaging about art's transformative power. As Cisco Bradley notes in his biography of the bassist, "Parker has been a community builder and a justice seeker throughout his life, believing his art and that of his collaborators to be imbued with transformative power to make the world a better place" (*Universal Tonality*, 7).

   3. Qtd. in Solnit, *A Paradise*, 131.

   4. Attali, *Noise*, 135.

   5. Wyman, *Defiant*, 145.

   6. Carras and Lewis, "A Gateway," 35.

   7. Carras and Lewis, "A Gateway," 32.

   8. Fischlin, Risk, and Stewart, "The Poetics," 1.

   9. King, *Where Do We Go*, 21.

   10. In May 2020, for example, a group of Black men in Louisville who were protesting police violence formed a human shield to protect a police officer who had been separated from the rest of his unit (see Duncan, "Black Men Form Human Shield": https://thegrio.com/2020/05/31/louisville-men-police-officer-protest).

   11. Loeb, "Coronavirus."

   12. Griffin, "Teaching."

   13. Roy, "The Pandemic."

   14. Davidson, "The Single."

   15. Davidson, "The Single."

   16. Fischlin and Porter, *Playing for Keeps*, 2.

   17. Fischlin and Porter, *Playing for Keeps*, 11.

Introduction

   1. Giroux, "Foreword," xi.

   2. In light of the Covid-19 pandemic, and as we think about some of the ways in which it has highlighted the role that improvisational practices can play in

modeling alternative ways of being together and collaborating in community, even while we remain apart, a related question emerges: how might cultural and pedagogical institutions that present and promote improvised music shape our understanding of (and potential responses to) future crises and their aftermath? For more on the role of improvisation as a generative model of pedagogical practice during the pandemic, see, Haseman, "Improvising Our Way": "Being able and willing to improvise," he writes, "is a central habit of mind for artists, designers and creative educators and in this extraordinary moment in the history of education, artists-educators are being asked to improvise like never before." See also, for example, Thompson, "Leon Teacher's Unscripted Theater"; Lavik, "Thermo"; as well as three issues (14.1 and 14.2–3) of *Critical Studies in Improvisation / Études critiques en improvisation* devoted to improvisation and the Covid-19 pandemic: "Improvisation, Musical Communities, and the COVID-19 Pandemic," coedited by Fischlin, Risk, and Stewart.

3. Cheng, *Just Vibrations*, 26.

4. Ellis, Adams, and Bochner, "Autoethnography," 284.

5. Ellis, Adams, and Bochner, "Autoethnography," 277.

6. The language in this summary is adapted from text provided by George Lewis for a grant proposal on which we collaborated.

7. See https://cjc.edu/jazzschool/intensives/summer-youth-programs/girls-jazz-blues-camp/ for more information. See also Tracy McMullen's discussion of the improvisative practices of middle and high school girls at the Girls' Jazz and Blues Camp in her essay "The Improvisative." For the Danish Jazz Camp for Girls, see https://www.danishjazz.com/jazz-camp-for-girls. See also Abend, "Girls Are Outnumbered."

8. Heble and Waterman, "Improvisation and Pedagogy."

9. Heble and Laver, *Improvisation and Music Education*, 1.

10. Ake, "Learning Jazz," 259.

11. Ake, "Learning Jazz," 258.

12. Ake, "Learning Jazz," 258.

13. Lasn, *Culture Jam*, xvii.

14. Lasn, *Culture Jam*, xi.

15. At a time when most classrooms have been forced to move online as a result of the Covid-19 pandemic, how might the idea, and the practice, of jamming the classroom take on new considerations? Does it, for example, become more difficult to topple power structures and use *détournement* when so much of the world is being filtered through and controlled by social media platforms and their algorithms? To what extent is it possible to subvert capitalist media culture when it is has now become central to survival for so many people?

16. Tomlinson and Lipsitz, *Insubordinate Spaces*, 14.

17. Tomlinson and Lipsitz, *Insubordinate Spaces*, 35.

18. We thank Will Cheng and Andrew Dell'Antonio for their thoughtful prompts and provocations on these matters.

19. Tomlinson and Lipsitz, *Insubordinate Spaces*, 36.

20. Tomlinson and Lipsitz, *Insubordinate Spaces*, 14.

21. Iyer, "Beneath Improvisation."

22. Iyer, "Beneath Improvisation."

23. Kelley, *Freedom Dreams*, 9.

24. Lewis, "Improvised Music after 1950," 94. In this important essay, Lewis writes about how the "sonic symbolism" associated with improvisation for African American musicians is "often constructed with a view toward social instrumentality. . . . New improvisative and compositional styles are often identified with ideals of race advancement and, more important, as resistive ripostes to perceived opposition to black social expression and economic advancement by the dominant white American culture" (94).

25. Bailey, *Improvisation*, xii.

26. Peters, *Improvising Improvisation*, 84. See also MacGlone and MacDonald: "It is important to note that the non-idiomatic nature of free improvisation remains a contentious issue more than two decades after Bailey's seminal text was published. For example, a contrasting view is that all improvised music is to some extent influenced by performers' backgrounds" ("Learning to Improvise," 279).

27. Peters, *Improvising Improvisation*, 84.

28. Qtd. in King, "Fire Music," 43.

29. Smith, "American Music," 111.

30. Qtd. from the "Support" page on the Creative Music Studio website. Accessed February 22, 2019. https://creativemusic.org/support/. See also Sweet, *Music Universe*.

31. See also Stó:lō scholar Dylan Robinson's "To All Who Should Be Concerned," a letter published in a special issue of *Intersections* devoted to "Decolonizing Music Pedagogies." The open letter describes important structural changes that Robinson feels are required in order for academics to engage in the urgent task of transforming "the unmarked, white supremacist, and settler colonial structures that guide our music education systems" (137). He contends that while diversifying the curriculum and hiring more Indigenous, Black, Latinx, Asian and other scholars of color (IBPOC) is one part of the change that's required to challenge current pedagogical structures and assumptions, these sorts of moves of "additive" inclusion can in fact maintain the larger system of white supremacy within which music programs operate" (137). What's needed instead, Robinson maintains, is the giving over of "space for IBPOC leadership to determine the parameters for change" (138).

32. Warwick, "Music Education."

33. Warwick, "Music Education."

34. Loveless, *How to Make Art*, 13.

35. Loveless, *How to Make Art*, 13.

36. Heewon Chang, Faith Ngunjiri, and Kathy-Ann Hernandez define collaborative autoethnography "as a qualitative research method in which researchers work in community to collect their autobiographical materials and to analyze and interpret their data collectively to gain a meaningful understanding of sociocultural phenomena reflected in their autobiographical data" (*Collaborative Autoethnography*, 24). Interestingly, they too make an explicit comparison between this research method and music: "AE [autoethnography] is to a solo performance as CAE [collaborative autoethnography] is to an ensemble. While the combination of instruments creates a unique musical piece, the success

of the composition [and, we would add, improvisation] is dependent on the authentic and unique contribution of each instrument. In CAE, each participant contributes to the collective work in his or her distinct and independent voice. At the same time, the combination of multiple voices to interrogate a social phenomena creates a unique synergy and harmony that autoethnographers cannot attain in isolation" (24).

37. Lugones and Spelman, "Have We Got a Theory," 573.

Chapter One

1. MacGlone and MacDonald, "Learning to Improvise," 281.
2. Lewis, "Improvisation and Pedagogy," 1.
3. Rollins interviewed by Marc Myers.
4. Rollins interviewed by Marc Myers.
5. Rollins interviewed by Marc Myers.
6. Rollins interviewed by Tavis Smiley.
7. Qtd. in Macnie, "Sonny Rollins."
8. Sawyer, *Group Genius*, xii.
9. We also recognize that it's important to ask broader questions about what or who supported Rollins during this time. What enabled him to spend up to fourteen hours a day practicing? In asking these questions, we note that such opportunities for creative self-exploration are not readily available to everyone (for example, people with large family responsibilities or who must work several jobs to survive).
10. Bakhtin, *Problems*, 293.
11. Okri, *A Way*, 46.
12. For a review of some of the literature on music and language, see Feld and Fox, "Music and Language." For an examination of the relationships between language and music cognition from a neuroscientific point of view, see Patel, *Music, Language.*
13. Adorno, "Music," 401.
14. Bailey, *Improvisation*, 106.
15. Adorno, "Music," 401.
16. While the emphasis on innovation certainly seems to be a core part of the discourse that surrounds free improvised music and other genres that reside in similar experimentalist constellations, we acknowledge there are many modes of improvisation in Europe and North America (and even more so in India, the Middle East, and elsewhere in the world) where manifest inventiveness may be undesirable because it occludes idiomatic specificity or negatively impacts the experience of dancers. This is the case, for instance, in some blues, some rock music, some R&B, gospel, baroque instrumental music, samba, forró, and even in some subgenres in jazz, among others.
17. Landgraf, *Improvisation as Art*, 24.
18. Extended techniques within contemporary Western art music traditions were being developed during the same period by musicians and composers working with notated music.

19. Qtd. in Bailey, *Improvisation*, 106.

20. Ake, "Learning Jazz," 260–61.

21. Ake, "Learning Jazz," 261.

22. Evan Parker, personal correspondence (email) with the authors, June 25, 2017.

23. Ake, "Learning Jazz," 261.

24. Independent record shops have been featured as vital pedagogical sites in the 2012 documentary film *Last Shop Standing* by Pip Piper, as well as in Rachel Joyce's 2017 novel *The Music Shop*. In the documentary, we're told that the independent record store is "a meeting place, almost like community centers." It's a place where people go to get "an education in music," where "nothing beats the buzz of meeting somebody face-to-face across the counter, and saying, 'Hey, have you heard this?'" In Joyce's novel, Frank, the owner of the independent record shop at the center of the narrative, has a knack for understanding the life situations of his customers and prescribing just the right music: "Frank had helped them [his customers] through illness, grief, loss of confidence and jobs, as well as the more daily things like football results and the weather. Not that he knew about all those things, but really it was a matter of listening, and he had endless patience" (Joyce, *The Music Shop*, 10).

25. In his book *Thinking in Jazz*, Paul Berliner has written about the way "aspiring players form relationships through a complex network of interrelated music centres that form the institutional infrastructure of the jazz community." Many of his comments seem relevant in the context of our arguments in this book: "Record shops, music stores, musicians' union halls, social clubs for the promotion of jazz, musicians' homes, booking agencies, practice studios, recording studios, and nightclubs," Berliner suggests, "all provide places where musicians interrelate with one another, and, to some extent, with fans. Amateur discographers and other devotees with extensive holdings of recordings, books, magazines, newsletters, films, and, more recently, video documentaries about jazz, act often as informal archivists for all or part of the community" (36–37).

26. Pauline Oliveros, personal correspondence (email) with the authors, January 28, 2015.

27. Dong-Won Kim, personal correspondence (email) with the authors, January 28, 2015.

28. Dong-Won Kim, personal correspondence (email) with the authors, January 28, 2015.

29. François Houle, personal correspondence (email) with the authors, May 20, 2015.

30. François Houle, personal correspondence (email) with the authors, May 20, 2015.

31. Bailey, *Improvisation*, 110.

32. Bailey, *Improvisation*, 110.

33. David Mott, personal correspondence (email) with the authors, January 24, 2015.

34. David Mott, personal correspondence (email) with the authors, January 24, 2015.

35. Bailey, *Improvisation*, 110.

36. Lewis, "Improvised Music," 110.

37. David Mott, personal correspondence (email) with the authors, January 24, 2015.

38. Lock, *Forces in Motion*, 27.

39. Csikszentmihalyi, *Flow*, 4.

40. William Parker, personal correspondence (email) with the authors, January 24, 2015.

41. Berkowitz, *The Improvising Mind*, xv.

42. Bailey, *Improvisation*, 110.

43. Lewis, "Teaching Improvised Music," 83.

Chapter Two

1. For a firsthand account of this encounter, see Crouch, *Kansas City Lightning*, 152–55.

2. Brody, "Getting Jazz Right."

3. In addition to the eleven interviews we specifically conducted for this chapter, we are drawing on interviews that have been done on other occasions: Jesse's previously published interview with Hamid Drake in *Cadence*, Ajay's public onstage interview with Douglas Ewart at the Guelph Jazz Festival Colloquium, Ajay's interview with Marianne Trudel as part of the Musical Improvisation at Land's End / Coin-du-Banc en folie project, Ajay's interview with Jane Bunnett when she took up the position as inaugural improviser-in-residence in Guelph, as well as interviews from the 1970s with soprano saxophonist Steve Lacy conducted by Derek Bailey and Brian Case (reprinted in and cited from Jason Weiss's book *Steve Lacy: Conversations*), and an interview that *"Fifteen" Questions* magazine conducted with trumpeter jaimie branch about improvisation. We also acknowledge our indebtedness to the methodologies and insights shared by Paul Berliner in his important book *Thinking in Jazz: The Infinite Art of Improvisation.* See, in particular, chapter two in Berliner, "Hanging Out and Jammin': The Jazz Community as an Educational System."

4. Stewart "Hamid Drake," 6.

5. Heble and Ewart, "A Total Community Embrace."

6. Kisliuk and Gross, "What's the 'It'?," 250.

7. Lewis, "Teaching," 98.

8. George Lewis, personal correspondence (email) with the authors, June 3, 2017.

9. George Lewis, personal correspondence (email) with the authors, June 3, 2017.

10. Iyer, "Improvisation," 171.

11. George Lewis, personal correspondence (email) with the authors, June 3, 2017.

12. George Lewis, personal correspondence (email) with the authors, June 3, 2017.

13. Fischlin, "Improvised Responsibility," 290.

14. Freire, *Pedagogy*, 80.

15. Lewis, *A Power*, 448.

16. Stewart, "Hamid Drake," 7.

17. Stewart, "Hamid Drake," 7.

18. We recognize that, while our interlocutors mostly share very positive experiences, not all musicians have had a positive experience of mentorship. Unfortunately, we continue to hear about improvisers, especially young women improvisers, whose relationships with their teachers have been far more vexed, and often emotionally or sexually abusive. See, for instance, Sasha Berliner's account of her experiences as documented in her "Open Letter."

19. George Lewis, personal correspondence (email) with the authors, June 3, 2017.

20. Heble and Ewart, "A Total Community Embrace," 29, 27.

21. Norman Adams, personal correspondence (email) with the authors, June 4, 2017.

22. Anne Bourne, personal correspondence (email) with the authors, June 6, 2017.

23. Susie Ibarra, personal correspondence (email) with the authors, June 28, 2017.

24. William Parker, personal correspondence (email) with the authors, June 23, 2017.

25. Éric Normand, personal correspondence (email) with the authors, June 1, 2017.

26. Jaron Freeman-Fox, personal correspondence (email) with the authors, June 9, 2017.

27. Hamid Drake, personal correspondence (email) with the authors, June 25, 2017. Don Cherry also features prominently as a kind of mentor figure in Steve Lacy's stories about learning to improvise. For instance, in an interview conducted by Brian Case in 1979 and reprinted in Jason Weiss's book *Steve Lacy: Conversations*, Lacy describes how, after Cherry's arrival in New York in 1959, they came to be fast friends. Lacy recounts how Cherry would say, "'Well let's play,' and I'd say, 'OK, what do you want to play?' And he'd say, 'No, let's just play.' This was revolutionary to me at the time because I was into Monk tunes, and thought you had to have a tune, a structure, and chord changes, the whole thing. He'd just play, and when he played it was really alive" (qtd. in Weiss, 87). Lacy tells us that Cherry's "way of going into the beyond and just taking off—to not worry about where you were coming from, but just to go—I wanted to be able to do that myself" (qtd. in Weiss, 87). See also Lacy's interview with Derek Bailey, originally a 1974 radio interview that was later included in Bailey's book *Improvisation* and more recently reprinted in Weiss.

28. Prévost's comments are in contrast to Evan Parker's comments about mentorship in Una MacGlone and Raymond MacDonald's essay, "Learning to Improvise, Improvising to Learn": "When you get to my stage," Parker explains, "there's some obligation to use your situation to advance the positions of other players that you feel are especially worthy of it . . . it's just a necessary part of being in a community, a community of players" (287).

29. Eddie Prévost, personal correspondence (email) with the authors, May 19, 2017.

30. In an essay titled "The Pedagogical Imperative of Music Improvisation," improvising trombonist Scott Thomson makes a similar argument, suggesting that "ongoing pedagogical engagement is a necessary trait of a responsive, responsible improviser" (1).

31. Scholarship on community music is also a valuable point of reference here. See, for one example, Lee Higgins, "The Creative Music Workshop," for a discussion of "the workshop as a touchstone through which openness, diversity, freedom, and tolerance flow" (330).

32. Heble and Ewart, "A Total Community Embrace," 30.

33. Branch quoted in *"Fifteen" Questions.*

34. Branch quoted in *"Fifteen" Questions.*

35. Heble and Bunnett, "Things That You Hope," 220.

36. Heble and Bunnett, "Things That You Hope," 231.

37. Trudel, in-person interview with Ajay Heble at Musical Improvisation at Land's End / Coin-du-Banc en folie, August 5–12, 2017.

38. Norman Adams, personal correspondence (email) with the authors, June 4, 2017.

39. Norman Adams, personal correspondence (email) with the authors, June 4, 2017.

40. Evan Parker, personal correspondence (email) with the authors, June 25, 2017.

41. Jean Derome, personal correspondence (email) with the authors, June 24, 2017.

42. William Parker, personal correspondence (email) with the authors, June 23, 2017.

43. Susie Ibarra, personal correspondence (email) with the authors, June 28, 2017.

44. Anne Bourne, personal correspondence (email) with the authors, June 6, 2017.

45. George Lewis, personal correspondence (email) with the authors, June 3, 2017.

46. Ake, "Learning Jazz," 258.

47. Ake, "Learning Jazz," 259.

48. Ake, "Learning Jazz," 259. Not apocryphal, but often embellished (see Crouch).

49. Lewis, "Teaching Improvised Music," 88.

50. Lewis, "Teaching Improvised Music," 89.

51. Lewis, personal correspondence (email) with the authors, June 3, 2017.

52. Norman Adams, personal correspondence (email) with the authors, June 4, 2017.

53. Anne Bourne, personal correspondence (email) with the authors, June 6, 2017.

54. Jean Derome, personal correspondence (email) with the authors, June 24, 2017.

55. Hamid Drake, personal correspondence (email) with the authors, June 25, 2017.

56. Jaron Freeman-Fox, personal correspondence (email) with the authors, June 9, 2017.

57. Susie Ibarra, personal correspondence (email) with the authors, June 28, 2017.

58. Normand, personal correspondence (email) with the authors, June 1, 2017.

59. William Parker, personal correspondence (email) with the authors, June 23, 2017.

60. Evan Parker, personal correspondence (email) with the authors, June 25, 2017.

61. Eddie Prévost, personal correspondence (email) with the authors, May 19, 2017.

Chapter Three

1. hooks, *Teaching Community*, 41.

2. See also Heble, *Classroom Action*, for discussion of issues around planning and design, grading and evaluation, and methods and practices related to community-based learning.

3. McCarthy and Crichlow, "Introduction," xxvii.

4. Sommer, *The Work of Art*, 7.

5. Sommer, *The Work of Art*, 102.

6. Wyman, *The Defiant Imagination*, 145.

7. Wynn, *Music/City*, 15.

8. Evans and Boyte, *Free Spaces*, 202.

9. See, for example, Heble, *Landing*; Fischlin, Heble, and Lipsitz, *The Fierce Urgency*; Stewart, "Freedom Music."

10. Lipsitz, *American Studies*, 229.

11. Quinn, "Arts Festivals," 937.

12. While our particular focus here is on festivals and presenters of improvised and more experimental forms of music, rather than on large-scale corporate-driven festivals, we acknowledge that there is an important body of research that has discussed and debated the corporatization of jazz and large-scale jazz festivals. Mark Laver's book *Jazz Sells: Music, Marketing, and Meaning*, for instance, provides a provocative analysis of "the deeply vexed—and seldom discussed—issue of jazz's circulation in a capitalist society and the culture of consumption" (3). Laver asks, "What is it about jazz that has made it appealing to advertisers and marketers as an advertising and branding tool?" (2). For Laver's discussion of the role of sponsorship in major Canadian jazz festivals, see, in particular, the chapter entitled "The Bank of Music." In his book *The Jazz Bubble*, Dale Chapman explores how the "invocation of jazz as a catalyst for economic growth [and] the contradictory role of profit-seeking in twenty-first-century philanthropy—suggest that the political economy of jazz has a great deal to tell us about the interconnections between culture, ideology, and socioeconomic conditions in an era of ascendant financial capital" (5). See also Regis and Walton, "Producing

the Folk." The New Orleans Jazz and Heritage Festival, suggest Regis and Walton, "is both a cultural icon and an economic powerhouse that wields corporate like power within the New Orleans economy and is even a recognizable power in the national and global music marketplaces. The festival's importance in the city's postindustrial economy cannot be overstated. Tourism is the lifeblood of this city, and Jazz Fest is big business. For local and regional performers and traditional artists, Jazz Fest is the gatekeeper to larger markets, and consequently (almost inevitably) it exerts a magnetic or even a distorting effect on local music and community traditions. And while Jazz Fest ideology and marketed authenticity remain rooted in folk reverence, festival practices often result in folk marginalization, as producers are enmeshed in the larger process of cultural commodification of music and arts in the global marketplace. The ideologies of Jazz Fest spring from a desire to create authentic representation of beloved traditions and the imagination to envision creating new social/racial possibilities. And the limitations of Jazz Fest rest on realpolitik, the everyday-ness of doing, and the power of the market" (401).

13. Lewis, "Teaching Improvised Music," 88.

14. See Jim Merod's comment in "Jazz as a Cultural Archive": "My sense is that the jazz archive . . . eludes any inclusive theory of its achievement. . . . One merely thinks of the suspicion of so many magnificent jazz musicians who find the rational neatness and intellectual sweep of large interpretive frameworks about jazz to have no organic relationship to their lives' experiences, to the rhythm of creation and travel and invention that, against all odds, characterizes their work" (6).

15. Wyman, *The Defiant Imagination*, 7.

16. Wyman, *The Defiant Imagination*, 82.

17. See Heble, *Landing*, 94–95.

18. Wyman, *The Defiant Imagination*, 102–3.

19. Parker and In Order to Survive, *The Peach Orchard*. The liner notes to the album remark that "In Order to Survive" (disc 2, track 8) is the band's theme song, in which they state their motto: "In order to survive, we must keep hope alive," which we've quoted here.

20. Quotation pulled from the 2004 version of the Vision Festival website, at the time found at www.visionfestival.org and accessed May 18, 2004. This site is no longer available online, but more information on the Arts for Art organization can be found at www.artsforart.org. More information on the Vision Festival, specifically, can be found at www.artsforart.org/vision/html

21. Quotation pulled from the 2004 version of the Vision Festival website, at the time found at www.visionfestival.org and accessed May 18, 2004.

22. Arts for Art, "Annual Report 2018."

23. Arts for Art, "Artists for a Free World," https://www.artsforart.org/advocacy.html

24. Parker, personal interview with Ajay Heble, Victoriaville, May 22, 2004.

25. Parker, personal interview with Ajay Heble, Victoriaville, May 22, 2004.

26. Zournazi, *Hope*, 274.

27. hooks, *Teaching Community*, 192.

28. Picard and Robinson, "Remaking Worlds," 14.

29. Picard and Robinson, "Remaking Worlds," 20.

30. Picard and Robinson, "Remaking Worlds," 26.

31. Foster, *Genuine Multiculturalism,* 41.

32. Ang, *On Not Speaking Chinese,* 193.

33. San Juan, *Racism and Cultural Studies,* 19.

34. Qtd. in Estrada, "UCSB."

35. Cooper, *Everyday Utopias,* 2.

36. Wynn, *Music/City,* 167–68.

37. Wynn, *Music/City,* 168.

38. Wynn, *Music/City,* 168.

39. Although not specifically about improvised forms of music making, this, in psychology, is known as a "musical peak experience" where "the music absorbs the listeners and shuts out everything else. It evokes strong emotions and a lot of other reactions, from purely physical responses to experiences of existential and spiritual character" (Whaley, Sloboda, and Gabrielsson, "Peak Experiences").

40. See also sociologist Howard Becker's suggestion, in his important book *Art Worlds*: "The heat in discussions of aesthetics usually exists because what is being decided is not only an abstract philosophical question but also some allocation of valuable resources. Whether jazz is really music or photography is really art, whether free-form jazz is really jazz and therefore music, whether fashion photographs are really photography and therefore art, are discussions, among other things, about whether people who play free-form jazz can perform in jazz clubs for the already existing jazz audience and whether fashion photographs can be exhibited and sold in important galleries and museums" (135).

41. In his analysis of place making in three American music festivals, Wynn acknowledges "the difficulty of fully comprehending and analyzing a complex and adaptable sociological phenomenon that involves thousands of people. On the one hand," he notes, "there are moments of cohesiveness—for example, for organizers who might rally around a certain vision of city marketing, or for audiences as they cycle through a particular spatial arrangement of activities. And yet, on the other hand, festivals can never wield complete control of the experiences and interactions of all participants. There are always incongruities and departures from the official narrative: from antagonistic or contrarian moments (e.g., attendees reacting to branding, locals bristling at the crowds, protestors picketing the event), to alternative activities that exist alongside official proceedings . . . to simple juxtapositions wherein two different people have very different experiences alongside each other" (244–45).

42. Boyer, Cook, and Steinberg, *Legible Practices,* 13–14.

43. Lewis, "Teaching Improvised Music," 94.

44. Lewis, "Teaching Improvised Music," 107.

45. See, for instance, Wilson, "A Rhapsody."

Chapter Four

1. Goldstein, "Improvisation," 9.

2. Goldstaub, "Opening the Door," 51.

3. Campbell and Higgins, *Free to Be Musical*, 2.

4. College Music Society, "Transforming Music Study," 5–6.

5. Ake, "Learning Jazz," 264.

6. Ake, "Learning Jazz," 264.

7. Monson, *Saying Something*, 5.

8. Monson, *Saying Something*, 193.

9. See, for example, Ferand, *Improvisation* and McGee, *Improvisation.*

10. For a fuller discussion of the diminished role of improvisation in Western art music, see Moore, "The Decline of Improvisation."

11. Of course, market interests were just one among many factors that shaped patterns of private and public music making in the nineteenth and early twentieth centuries, including the ebb and flow of interest in improvisation within Western art music traditions. For a fuller discussion of these trends, see Gooley, *Fantasies of Improvisation* and Stewart, "Intervections."

12. Qtd. in Fischlin and Heble, *The Other Side*, 16.

13. Fischlin and Heble, *The Other Side*, 16.

14. Oliveros, "Harmonic Anatomy," 53.

15. Uitti, "Preserving the Scelsi Improvisations," 12–14.

16. Lewis, "Improvised Music," 92.

17. See Nettl, "Thoughts on Improvisation." For a more detailed literature review of important essays on improvisation, please see Lewis and Piekut's "Introduction."

18. Qtd. in Ake, *Jazz Cultures*, 1.

19. See http://www.improvcommunity.ca/projects/toolkit

20. Sarath, "Founder's Message."

21. Lewis, "Teaching Improvised Music," 79.

22. Lewis, "Teaching Improvised Music," 79.

23. I (Stewart) discuss this course in an essay titled "Improvisation Pedagogy in Theory and Practice." The discussion here reprints portions of that chapter.

24. Evans and Boyte, *Free Spaces*, 2.

25. Said, *Representations of the Intellectual*, xvii.

26. Lewis, "Collaborative Improvisation," 46.

Chapter Five

1. While her comments here point to improvisation's potential for positive change, Waterman did not, in her rejoinder to William Parker during this Q and A session, intend to express an uncritical utopian view. Throughout her conversations with us, Waterman has been quick to note that improvisation can also function as a potential agent of harm.

2. Sommer, *The Work of Art*, 7.

3. Higgins, *Community Music*, 4.

4. Higgins, *Community Music*, 4.

5. Lewis, "Improvisation and Pedagogy," 2.

6. Giroux, "Foreword," xi.

7. United Nations, *Plan of Action*, 46; our emphasis.

8. See Heble et al., "Improvisation as Pedagogy" for more details and analysis of the research conducted during this initial phase of the project.

9. Several research team members, student interns, and graduate research assistants have been involved with this project over the years. Heather Granger, Ellen Waterman, Elizabeth Jackson, Rob Jackson, and Melissa Walker deserve special mention. We are grateful to them for their engagement with this partnered research initiative.

10. Clements, "The Evaluation."

11. Madyaningrum and Sonn, "Exploring the Meaning."

12. De Quadros and Dorstewitz, "Community."

13. Varvarigou et al., "Bringing Different Generations Together."

14. Guetzkow, "How the Arts Impact Communities."

15. Lubet, "The Inclusion of Music," 729.

16. Higgins, *Community Music*, 172.

17. Heble et al., "Improvisation as Pedagogy," 10.

18. Heble et al., "Improvisation as Pedagogy," 10.

19. Heble et al., "Improvisation as Pedagogy," 10–11.

20. Granger et al., "So What's Research Got to Do with It?"

21. Heble et al., "Improvisation as Pedagogy," 11–12.

22. Baskin, "Perfect Harmony."

23. Barbara Sellers, personal correspondence (email) with Ajay Heble, March 2, 2016.

24. The films are available for viewing on the IICSI website, at http://improvisationinstitute.ca/news/stories-of-impact/

25. The artists who have facilitated "Play Who You Are" workshops have included Rich Marsella, Matana Roberts, and Rob Wallace (2008), Jane Bunnett and Larry Cramer (2009, 2011), Nicolas Caloia and members of the Ratchet Orchestra (2010), Scott Thomson and Susanna Hood (2012), Rich Marsella (2013), Jesse Stewart (2014), Laura Stinson (2015), Rich Burrows and Joe Sorbara (2016), Joe Sorbara and Lynette Segal (2017), and SlowPitchSound (2018).

26. Costa-Giomi, "Music Instruction" and "The Long-Term Effects"; Črnčec, Wilson, and Prior, "The Cognitive and Academic Benefits"; Rauscher and Hinton, "Music Instruction."

27. A 2019 documentary titled *Rich Tapestries: The Ongoing Story of* WAAM, includes some footage of the *Mud Lake Symphony* project. See https://vimeo.com/307959990

28. For more thorough discussions of the Adaptive Use Musical Instrument, see Oliveros et al., "A Musical Improvisation Interface," and Stewart et al., "AUMI-Futurism."

29. The video is available at https://vimeo.com/114442912

30. Huggett et al., "Turning the Page."

31. Parić, "Biopsychological Effects."

32. Parić, "Biopsychological Effects," 64.

33. Parić, "Biopsychological Effects," 63.

34. Parić, "Biopsychological Effects," 63.

35. Parić, "Biopsychological Effects," 62.

36. Parić, "Biopsychological Effects," 63.

37. Parić, "Biopsychological Effects," 63.

38. At the time of this writing, there have been four editions of the camp. The first two iterations have been featured in documentary films: Kimber Sider's *Musical Improvisation at Land's End / Coin-du-Banc en folie* is available online at http://improvisationinstitute.ca/document/musical-improvisation-at-lands-end-coin-du-banc-en-folie-official-selection/. João França's *Why I'm Here / Pourquoi je suis ici* is available at http://improvisationinstitute.ca/document/why-im-here/

39. See https://www.cjecotedegaspe.ca/place-aux-jeunes: "Place aux jeunes est un programme d'envergure nationale mis sur pied afin de contrer l'exode des jeunes en région. Comme la région de la Gaspésie et des Îles-de-la-Madeleine ne dispose pas d'université sur son territoire, plusieurs jeunes quittent la région pour s'établir dans les grands centres urbains afin de poursuivre leurs études et décident parfois d'y demeurer une fois leurs études terminées. Ainsi, la Gaspésie perd chaque année un bon nombre de jeunes finissants qui auraient pu mettre leurs connaissances au profit de la région et ainsi participer à son développement socioéconomique."

40. Salzman, "What's Next?"

41. Higgins, *Community Music*, 5.

42. Higgins, *Community Music*, 5.

43. Roberts quoted in Ham, "Matana Roberts."

44. Foster, *Genuine Multiculturalism*, 41.

45. Ang, *On Not Speaking Chinese*, 193.

46. The Improvisation Tool Kit is available at http://www.improvcommunity.ca/projects/toolkit

47. Granger et al., "So What's Research Got to Do with It?"

48. Granger et al., "So What's Research Got to Do with It?"

49. Fischlin, "Improvised Responsibility," 293.

Coda

1. Grubbs, *Now That the Audience Is Assembled*, 135.

2. Grubbs, *Now That the Audience Is Assembled*, 135–36.

3. Giroux, "Foreword," xi.

4. Said, *Humanism*, 75.

5. Said, *Humanism*, 75.

6. Said, *Humanism*, 76.

7. Grubbs, *Now That the Audience Is Assembled*, 58.

8. Lewis, "Improvisation and Pedagogy," 1.

9. Dimitriadis, "Pedagogy," 296.

10. Dimitriadis, "Pedagogy."

11. Dimitriadis, "Pedagogy."

12. This is taken from the description on the back cover of Grubbs's book.

13. Lipsitz, *American Studies*, 276.

14. Lipsitz, *American Studies*, 277.

15. Lipsitz, *American Studies,* 229.

16. Dove, "The Music," 196.

17. Thomson, "The Pedagogical Imperative."

18. Oliveros, liner notes, *Crone Music,* Lovely Music, LCD 1903, 1990, compact disc.

19. See also performance artist and poet David Antin's book *Tuning* for another description of the transformations facilitated by a performance by Pauline Oliveros. Antin describes a memorial service during which Oliveros engages those assembled in an interactive performance that allows them to process their grief as members of a community: "all around the room / people were crying and smiling and singing in / waves of sound that throbbed and swelled and ebbed / and climbed and peaked and dropped away into a / silence that lasted until Pauline thanked everyone / because the piece was over" (2).

20. A recording of the anniversary concert was made and released in 2014 under the title *Dunrobin Sonic Gems,* a pun on Dunrobin Sonic Gym, where the concert and recording took place.

21. Grubbs, *Now That the Audience Is Assembled,* 135.

Works Cited

Abend, Lisa. "Girls Are Outnumbered in Jazz. At This Summer Camp, They Run the Show." *New York Times*, July 7, 2022. https://www.nytimes.com/2022/07/07/arts/music/jazz-camp-for-girls.html

Adorno, Theodor W. "Music, Language, and Composition." Translated by Susan Gillespie. *Musical Quarterly* 77, no. 3 (1993): 401–14.

Ake, David. *Jazz Cultures.* Berkeley: University of California Press, 2002.

Ake, David. "Learning Jazz, Teaching Jazz." In *The Cambridge Companion to Jazz,* edited by Mervyn Cooke and David Horn, 255–69. New York: Cambridge University Press, 2002.

Anderson, Maureen. "The White Reception of Jazz in America." *African American Review* 38, no. 1 (2004): 135–46.

Ang, Ien. *On Not Speaking Chinese: Living Between Asia and the West.* London: Routledge, 2001.

Antin, David. *Tuning.* New York: New Directions, 1984.

Arts for Art. "Annual Report 2018." September 13, 2018. https://issuu.com/artsforart/docs/annual_reports_final_issue_upload_f

Arts for Art. "Artists for a Free World." Accessed March 4, 2019. https://www.artsforart.org/advocacy.html

Attali, Jacques, *Noise: The Political Economy of Music.* Translated by Brian Massumi. Minneapolis: University of Minnesota Press, 1985.

Bailey, Derek. *Improvisation: Its Nature and Practice in Music.* New York: Da Capo, 1993.

Bakhtin, Mikhail. *Problems of Dostoevsky's Poetics.* Edited and translated by Caryl Emerson. Minneapolis: University of Minneapolis Press, 1984.

Baskin, Amy. "Perfect Harmony." *Today's Parent* (blog). September 13, 2009.

Becker, Howard. *Art Worlds.* 25th Anniversary Edition. Berkeley: University of California Press, 2008.

Berklee Institute of Jazz and Gender Justice. Berklee College of Music. Accessed January 12, 2023. https://college.berklee.edu/jazz-gender-justice

Berkowitz, Aaron. *The Improvising Mind: Cognition and Creativity in the Musical Moment.* New York: Oxford University Press, 2010.

Berliner, Paul. *Thinking in Jazz: The Infinite Art of Improvisation.* Chicago: University of Chicago Press, 1994.

Berliner, Sasha. "Open Letter to Ethan Iverson (and the Rest of Jazz Patriarchy)." Originally published at SashaBerlinerMusic.com and available online at https://static1.squarespace.com/static/58bf64e6c534a5e3ac61401d/t/5a 3cacc4e4966be9b63ec7f4/1513925836404/BerlinerSashaAnOpenLetter .pdf. Accessed January 12, 2023.

Borgo, David. "Free Jazz in the Classroom: An Ecological Approach to Music Education." *Jazz Perspectives* 1, no. 1 (2007): 61–88.

Boyer, Bryan, Justin W. Cook, and Marco Steinberg. *Legible Practices: Six Stories about the Craft of Stewardship.* Sitra, 2013. http://helsinkidesignlab.org/peopl epods/themes/hdl/downloads/Legible_Practises.pdf

Bradley, Cisco. *Universal Tonality: The Life and Music of William Parker.* Durham, NC: Duke University Press, 2021.

branch, jaimie. "jaimie branch of Anteloper about Improvisation." *"Fifteen" Questions.* Accessed January 12, 2023. https://www.15questions.net/interview/jai mie-branch-anteloper-about-improvisation/page-1/

Brody, Richard. "Getting Jazz Right in the Movies." *New Yorker.* October 13, 2014. http://www.newyorker.com/culture/richard-brody/whiplash-getting-jazz-ri ght-movies

Campbell, Patricia Shehan, David Myers, and Ed Sarath [College Music Society]. "Transforming Music Study from Its Foundations: A Manifesto for Progressive Change in the Undergraduate Preparation of Music Majors." *College Music Symposium* 56 (2016): i–22.

Campbell, Patricia Shehan, and Lee Higgins. *Free to Be Musical: Group Improvisation in Music.* Plymouth, UK: Rowman and Littlefield, 2010.

Carras, Christos, and Eric Lewis. "'A Gateway between One World and the Next': Performance-Based Arts in Covid Times." In *Pandemic Societies,* edited by Jean-Louis Denis, Catherine Régis, and Daniel Weinstock, with the collaboration of Clara Champagne, 30–53. Montreal: McGill-Queen's University Press, 2021.

Chang, Heewon, Faith Ngunjiri, and Kathy-Ann Hernandez. *Collaborative Autoethnography.* Walnut Creek, CA: Left Coast Press, 2013.

Chapman, Dale. *The Jazz Bubble: Neoclassical Jazz in Neoliberal Culture.* Oakland: University of California Press, 2018.

Chazelle, Damien (dir.). *Whiplash.* 2014.

Cheng, William. *Just Vibrations: The Purpose of Sounding Good.* Ann Arbor: University of Michigan Press, 2016.

Clements, Paul. "The Evaluation of Community Arts Projects and the Problems with Social Impact Methodology." *International Journal of Art & Design Education* 26, no. 3 (2007): 325–35.

Cooper, Davina. *Everyday Utopias: The Conceptual Life of Promising Spaces.* Durham, NC: Duke University Press, 2014.

Costa-Giomi, Eugenia. "The Long-Term Effects of Childhood Music Instruction on Intelligence and General Cognitive Abilities." *Update: Applications of Research in Music Education* 33, no. 2 (2014): 20–26.

Costa-Giomi, Eugenia. "Music Instruction and Children's Intellectual Development: The Educational Context of Music Participation." In *Music, Health, and*

Wellbeing, edited by Raymond MacDonald, Gunter Kreutz, and Laura Mitchell, 339–55. Oxford: Oxford University Press, 2013.

Črnčec, Rudi, Sarah J. Wilson, and Margot Prior. "The Cognitive and Academic Benefits of Music to Children: Facts and Fiction." *Educational Psychology* 26, no. 4 (2006): 579–94.

Crouch, Stanley. *Kansas City Lightning: The Rise and Times of Charlie Parker.* New York: Harper, 2013.

Csikszentmihalyi, Mihaly. *Flow: The Psychology of Optimal Experience.* New York: Harper & Row. 1990.

Davidson, Cathy, "The Single Most Essential Requirement in Designing a Fall Online Course." *HASTAC.* May 11, 2020. https://www.hastac.org/blogs/cat hy-davidson/2020/05/11/single-most-essential-requirement-designing-fall -online-course

De Quadros, Andr, and Philipp Dorstewitz. "Community, Communication, Social Change: Music in Dispossessed Indian Communities." *International Journal of Community Music* 41, no. 1 (2011): 59–70.

Dias, José, and Anton Hunter. "The Noise Indoors: Improvisation, Community, and #StayHome." *Critical Studies in Improvisation / Études critiques en improvisation* 14, nos. 2–3 (2021). https://doi.org/10.21083/csieci.v14i2.6335

Dimitriadis, Greg. "Pedagogy on the Move: New Intersections in (between) the Educative and the Performative." In *The Sage Handbook of Performance Studies,* edited by D. Soyini Madison and Judith Hamera, 296–308. Thousand Oaks, CA: Sage, 2006. https://dx.doi.org/10.4135/9781412976145.n16

Dove, David. "The Music Is the Pedagogy." In *Improvisation and Music Education: Beyond the Classroom,* edited by Ajay Heble and Mark Laver, 183–97. New York: Routledge, 2016.

Duncan, Nicole. "Black Men Form Human Shield to Protect Police Officer During Protest." *The Grio.* May 31, 2020. https://thegrio.com/2020/05/31/louis ville-men-police-officer-protest/

Ellis, Carolyn, Tony E. Adams, and Arthur P. Bochner. "Autoethnography: An Overview." *Historical Social Research* 36, no. 4 (2011): 273–90.

Estrada, Andrea. "UCSB Black Studies Scholar Examines Improvisation as a Tool for Social Change." *UC Santa Barbara Current.* July 10, 2013. https://www.ne ws.ucsb.edu/2013/013580/ucsb-black-studies-scholar-examines-improvisati on-tool-social-change

Evans, Sara, and Harry Boyte. *Free Spaces: The Sources of Democratic Change in America.* New York: Harper & Row, 1986.

Ewell, Philip, "Music Theory's White Racial Frame." *Music Theory Spectrum* 43, no. 2 (2021): 1–6. https://doi.org/10.1093/mts/mtaa031

Feld, Steven, and Aaron A. Fox. "Music and Language." *Annual Review of Anthropology* 23 (1994): 25–53.

Ferand, E. T. *Improvisation in Nine Centuries of Western Music.* Cologne: ArnoVolk Verlag, 1961.

Fischlin, Daniel. "Improvised Responsibility: Opening Statements—(Call and) Responsibility: Improvisation, Ethics, Co-creation." In *The Improvisation Studies Reader: Spontaneous Acts,* edited by Rebecca Caines and Ajay Heble, 289–95. New York: Routledge, 2015.

Fischlin, Daniel, and Ajay Heble, eds. *The Other Side of Nowhere: Jazz, Improvisa-*

tion, and Communities in Dialogue. Middletown, CT: Wesleyan University Press, 2004.

Fischlin, Daniel, Ajay Heble, and George Lipsitz. *The Fierce Urgency of Now: Improvisation, Rights, and the Ethics of Cocreation.* Durham, NC: Duke University Press, 2013.

Fischlin, Daniel, and Eric Porter. *Playing for Keeps: Improvisation in the Aftermath.* Durham, NC: Duke University Press, 2020.

Fischlin, Daniel, Laura Risk, and Jesse Stewart, eds. "Improvisation, Musical Communities, and the COVID-19 Pandemic." Special issues of *Critical Studies in Improvisation / Études critiques en improvisation* 14, no. 1, 2–3 (2021).

Foster, Cecil. *Genuine Multiculturalism: The Tragedy and Comedy of Diversity.* Montreal: McGill-Queen's University Press, 2014.

Freire, Paulo. *Pedagogy of the Oppressed.* Translated by Myra Bergman Ramos. 30th Anniversary Edition. New York: Continuum, 2005.

Giroux, Henry. "Foreword: Contending Zones and Public Spaces." In *Zones of Contention: Essays on Art, Institutions, Gender, and Anxiety,* edited by Carol Becker, ix–xii. Albany: State University of New York Press, 1996.

Goldstaub, Paul. "Opening the Door to Classroom Improvisation: Experimenting with Sound, Rhythm, Language, Visual Stimuli, and Form Can Lay the Groundwork for Creative Improvisation." *Music Educators Journal* 82, no. 5 (1996): 45–51.

Goldstein, Malcolm. "Improvisation: Towards a Whole Musician in a Fragmented Society (1983)." In *Sounding the Full Circle: Concerning Music Improvisation and Other Related Matters.* Sheffield, VT: Malcolm Goldstein (self-published), 1988. http://frogpeak.org/unbound/goldstein/goldstein_fullcircle.pdf

Gooley, Dana. *Fantasies of Improvisation: Free Playing in Nineteenth-Century Music.* New York: Oxford University Press, 2018.

Granger, Heather, Elizabeth Jackson, Rob Jackson, Ellen Ringler, and Rob Wallace. "So What's Research Got to Do with It? Sharing Findings of Short- and Long-Term Research into Community Improvisation." Panel presentation at the 2017 Guelph Jazz Festival Colloquium, "Partnering for Change: Learning outwards from Jazz and Improvisation," September 13–15, 2017, Guelph, ON, Canada.

Grantham, Jim. *The Jazzmaster Cookbook.* Oakland, CA: Nightbird Music, 1995.

Griffin, Farah Jasmine, "Teaching African American Literature during COVID-19." *Boston Review.* May 21, 2020. http://bostonreview.net/arts-society/farah-jasmine-griffin-teaching-african-american-literature-during-covid-19

Grubbs, David. *Now That the Audience Is Assembled.* Durham, NC: Duke University Press, 2018.

Guetzkow, Joshua. "How the Arts Impact Communities: An Introduction to the Literature on Arts Impact Studies." "Taking the Measure of Culture" Conference, Princeton University, June 7–8, 2002. https://www.princeton.edu/~artspol/workpap/WP20%20-%20Guetzkow.pdf

Ham, Robert. "Matana Roberts on 'Panoramic Soundquilting,' Living on a Boat, and Exploring the South." *Paste.* February 13, 2015. https://www.pastemagazine.com/music/matana-roberts-on-panoramic-soundquilting-living-o/

Haseman, Brad. "Improvising Our Way beyond Emergency Remote Teaching."

Kadenze. April 1, 2020. https://blog.kadenze.com/digital-learning/improvising-our-way-beyond-emergency-remote-teaching/

Heble, Ajay, ed. *Classroom Action: Human Rights, Critical Activism, and Community-Based Education*. Toronto: University of Toronto Press, 2017.

Heble, Ajay. "Diversifying the Base of Valued Knowledges: Jazz, Improvisation, and the Cultural Politics of Arts Presentation." In *Pluralism in the Arts in Canada: A Change Is Gonna Come*, edited by Charles C. Smith, 23–28. Ottawa: Canadian Centre for Policy Alternatives, 2012.

Heble, Ajay. *Landing on the Wrong Note: Jazz, Dissonance, and Critical Practice*. New York: Routledge, 2000.

Heble, Ajay. "Take Two / Rebel Musics: Human Rights, Resistant Sounds, and the Politics of Music Making." In *Rebel Musics: Human Rights, Resistant Sounds, and the Politics of Music Making*, edited by Daniel Fischlin and Ajay Heble, 232–48. Montreal: Black Rose, 2003.

Heble, Ajay, and Douglas Ewart. "A Total Community Embrace: Douglas R. Ewart in Conversation with Ajay Heble." In *Douglas R. Ewart's Crepuscule: Stories of Impact*, edited by Ajay Heble, 17–31. Guelph: International Institute for Critical Studies in Improvisation and PS Guelph, 2018.

Heble, Ajay, and Jane Bunnett. "'Things That You Hope a Human Being Will Be': Jane Bunnett in Conversation with Ajay Heble." In *Improvisation and Music Education: Beyond the Classroom*, edited by Ajay Heble and Mark Laver, 213–31. New York: Routledge, 2016.

Heble, Ajay, Rob Jackson, Melissa Walker, Ellen Waterman, and Ashlee Cunsolo Willox. "Improvisation as Pedagogy for Youth on the Margins." *Improvisation, Community, and Social Practice*. August 24, 2010. http://www.improvcommunity.ca/research/improvisation-pedagogy-youth-margins

Heble, Ajay, and Mark Laver, eds. *Musical Improvisation and Pedagogy: Beyond the Classroom*. New York: Routledge, 2016.

Heble, Ajay, and Ellen Waterman, eds. "Improvisation and Pedagogy." Special issue of *Critical Studies in Improvisation / Études critiques en improvisation* 3, no. 2 (2007). https://www.criticalimprov.com/index.php/csieci/issue/view/40

Heble, Ajay, and Ellen Waterman. "Sounds of Hope, Sounds of Change: Improvisation, Pedagogy, Social Justice." *Critical Studies in Improvisation / Études critiques en improvisation* 3, no. 2 (2007). https://www.criticalimprov.com/index.php/csieci/article/view/409/620

Higgins, Lee. *Community Music: In Theory and In Practice*. New York: Oxford University Press, 2012.

Higgins, Lee. "The Creative Music Workshop: Event, Facilitation, Gift." *International Journal of Music Education* 26, no. 4 (2008): 326–38.

hooks, bell. *Teaching Community: A Pedagogy of Hope*. New York: Routledge, 2004.

Huggett, J., A. Hall, L. Margita, D. Ratcliffe, L. Roswell, and J. Stewart. "Turning the Page on Disability and the Arts." Panel presentation at Power of the Arts National Forum, Carleton University, Ottawa, November 9, 2014.

Iyer, Vijay. "Beneath Improvisation." In *The Oxford Handbook of Critical Concepts in Music Theory*, edited by Alexander Rehding and Steven Rings. Oxford Handbooks Online, 2019.

Iyer, Vijay. "Improvisation: Terms and Conditions." In *Arcana IV: Musicians on Music*, edited by John Zorn, 171–75. New York: Hips Road / Tzadik, 2009.

Jazz Camp for Girls. Danish Jazz. Accessed January 12, 2023. https://www.danish jazz.com/jazz-camp-for-girls

Johansen, Gura Gravem, Kari Holdhus, Christina Larsson, and Una MacGlone. *Expanding the Space for Improvisation Pedagogy in Music: A Transdisciplinary Approach.* London: Routledge, 2019.

Joyce, Rachel. *The Music Shop.* Toronto: Anchor Canada, 2018. Originally published by Bond Street Books, 2017.

Kelley, Robin D. G. *Freedom Dreams: The Black Radical Imagination.* Boston: Beacon, 2002.

King, Daniel. "Fire Music: Lincoln Center Thaws Its Cold War on Jazz Activism." *Village Voice* 48, no. 11 (March 12–18, 2003): 42–43.

King, Martin Luther, Jr. *Where Do We Go from Here: Chaos or Community?* Boston: Beacon, 1967.

Kisliuk, Michelle, and Kelly Gross. "What's the 'It' That We Learn to Perform? Teaching BaAka Music and Dance." In *Performing Ethnomusicology: Teaching and Representation in World Music Ensembles*, edited by Ted Solis, 249–60. Los Angeles: University of California Press, 2004.

Landgraf, Edgar. *Improvisation as Art: Conceptual Challenges, Historical Perspectives.* New York: Continuum, 2011.

Lasn, Kalle. *Culture Jam: the Uncooling of America.* New York: Eagle Brook, 1999.

Laver, Mark. *Jazz Sells: Music, Marketing, and Meaning.* New York: Routledge, 2015.

Lavik, Erin. "Thermo in the Time of COVID-19: Using Improvisation to Foster Discussion and Translating the Experience to Online Learning." *Biomedical Engineering Education* 1 (2021): 133–38. https://doi.org/10.1007/s43683-020 -00022-z

LeFanu, Nicola. "Master Musician: An Impregnable Taboo?" *Contact* 31 (1987): 4–8.

Levine, Lawrence. *Highbrow/Lowbrow: The Emergence of Cultural Hierarchy in America.* Cambridge, MA: Harvard University Press, 1988.

Levine, Mark. *The Jazz Theory Book.* Petaluma, CA: Sher Music, 1995.

Lewis, George E. "Afterword to 'Improvised Music after 1950': The Changing Same." In *The Other Side of Nowhere: Jazz, Improvisation, and Communities in Dialogue*, edited by Daniel Fischlin and Ajay Heble, 163–72. Middletown, CT: Wesleyan University Press, 2004.

Lewis, George E. "Collaborative Improvisation as Critical Pedagogy." *Nka: Journal of Contemporary African Art* 34 (Spring 2014): 41–47.

Lewis, George E. "Improvisation and Pedagogy: Background and Focus of Inquiry." *Critical Studies in Improvisation / Études critiques en improvisation* 3, no. 2 (2007). https://www.criticalimprov.com/index.php/csieci/article/vi ew/412/659

Lewis, George E. "Improvised Music after 1950: Afrological and Eurological Perspectives." *Black Music Research Journal* 16, no. 1 (1996): 91–122.

Lewis, George E. "Keynote Address: Partnering Diversity." Keynote address at the Canadian New Music Network Forum, January 7–9, 2019, Halifax, Nova Scotia.

Lewis, George E. *A Power Stronger Than Itself: The AACM and American Experimental Music.* Chicago: University of Chicago Press, 2008.

Lewis, George E. "Teaching Improvised Music: An Ethnographic Memoir." In *Arcana: Musicians on Music*, edited by John Zorn, 78–109. New York: Granary, 2000.

Lewis, George, and Benjamin Piekut. *The Oxford Handbook of Critical Improvisation Studies*. Vol. 1. New York: Oxford University Press, 2016.

Lipsitz, George. *American Studies in a Moment of Danger*. Minneapolis: University of Minnesota Press, 2001.

Lock, Graham. *Forces in Motion: Anthony Braxton and the Meta-reality of Creative Music*. 30th Anniversary Edition. New York: Dover, 2018.

Loeb, Paul. "Coronavirus as a Teachable Classroom Moment: Engaging Students across the Curriculum." Campus Election Engagement Project. Accessed May 28, 2021. https://campuselect.org/coronavirus-as-a-teachable-classroom -moment-engaging-students-across-the-curriculum/

Loveless, Natalie. *How to Make Art at the End of the World: A Manifesto for Research-Creation*. Durham, NC: Duke University Press, 2019.

Lubet, Alex. "The Inclusion of Music / The Music of Inclusion." *International Journal of Inclusive Education* 13, no. 7 (2009): 727–39.

Lugones, Maria, and Elizabeth Spelman. "Have We Got a Theory for You! Feminist Theory, Cultural Imperialism and the Demand for 'the Woman's Voice.'" *Women's Studies International Forum* 6, no. 1 (1983): 573–81.

MacGlone, Una, and Raymond MacDonald. "Learning to Improvise, Improvising to Learn: A Qualitative Study of Learning Processes in Improvising Musicians." In *Distributed Creativity: Collaboration and Improvisation in Contemporary Music*, edited by Eric Clark and Mark Doffman, 278–94. New York: Oxford University Press, 2017.

Macnie, Jim. "Sonny Rollins Talks John Coltrane." *Lament for a Straight Line* (blog). September 7, 2011. https://lamentforastraightline.wordpress.com /tag/ornette-coleman/

Madyaningrum, Monica, and Christopher Sonn. "Exploring the Meaning of Participation in a Community Arts Project: A Case Study on the Seeming Project." *Journal of Community and Applied Social Psychology* 21, no. 4 (2011): 358–70.

Martenson, Jan. "The United Nations and Human Rights Today and Tomorrow." In *Human Rights in the Twenty-First Century: A Global Challenge*, edited by Kathleen E. Mahoney and Paul Mahoney, 925–36. Dordrecht: Martinus Nijhoff, 1993.

McCarthy, Cameron, and Warren Crichlow. "Introduction: Theories of Identity, Theories of Representation, Theories of Race." In *Race, Identity, and Representation in Education*, edited by Cameron McCarthy and Warren Crichlow, xiii–xxix. New York: Routledge, 1993.

McGee, Timothy, ed. *Improvisation in the Arts of the Middle Ages and Renaissance*. Kalamazoo, MI: Medieval Institute Publications, 2003.

McMullen, Tracy. "The Improvisative." In *The Oxford Handbook of Critical Improvisation Studies*, vol. 1, edited by George E. Lewis and Benjamin Piekut, 115–27. New York: Oxford University Press, 2016.

Merod, Jim, "Jazz as a Cultural Archive." *boundary* 2, no. 22 (summer 1995): 1–18.

Monson, Ingrid. *Saying Something: Jazz Improvisation and Interaction*. Chicago: University of Chicago Press, 1996.

Moore, Robin. "The Decline of Improvisation in Western Art Music: An Interpretation of Change." *International Review of the Aesthetics and Sociology of Music* 23, no. 1 (1992): 61–84.

Nettl, Bruno. "Thoughts on Improvisation: A Comparative Approach." *Musical Quarterly* 60 (1974): 1–19.

Okri, Ben. *A Way of Being Free.* London: Phoenix House, 1997.

Oliveros, Pauline. "Harmonic Anatomy: Women in Improvisation." In *The Other Side of Nowhere: Jazz, Improvisation, and Communities in Dialogue,* edited by Daniel Fischlin and Ajay Heble, 50–70. Middletown, CT: Wesleyan University Press, 2004.

Oliveros, Pauline, Leaf Miller, Jaclyn Heyen, Gillian Siddall, and Sergia Hazard. "A Musical Improvisation Interface for People with Severe Physical Disabilities." *Music and Medicine Journal* 3, no. 3 (2011): 172–81.

Parić, Angela. "Biopsychological Effects of Social Participation on Aging: The Role of Identity-Affirming Music and the Arts." PhD diss., Carleton University, 2019.

Parker, William. Liner notes to *Anagram* by David Mott and Jesse Stewart. Art Stew Records (679444005171), 2014, compact disc.

Parker, William, and In Order to Survive. *The Peach Orchard.* AUM Fidelity, AUM010/11, 1998, compact disc.

Patel, Aniruddh. *Music, Language and the Brain.* Oxford: Oxford University Press, 2007.

Peters, Gary. *Improvising Improvisation: From out of Philosophy, Music, Dance, and Literature.* Chicago: University of Chicago Press, 2017.

Picard, David, and Mike Robinson. "Remaking Worlds: Festivals, Tourism and Change." In *Festivals, Tourism and Social Change: Remaking Worlds,* edited by David Picard and Mike Robinson, 1–31. Clevedon: Channel View Publications, 2006.

Piper, Pip (dir.). *Last Shop Standing: The Rise, Fall and Rebirth of the Independent Record Shop.* Blue Hippo Media, 2012.

"Place aux jeunes." *Carrefour Jeunesse-Emploi MRC Côte-de-Gaspé.* Accessed June 6, 2020. https://www.cjecotedegaspe.ca/place-aux-jeunes

Prouty, Ken. "The 'Finite' Art of Improvisation: Pedagogy and Power in Jazz Improvisation." *Critical Studies in Improvisation / Études critiques en improvisation* 4, no. 1 (2008). https://www.criticalimprov.com/index.php/csieci/article/view/346/966

Prouty, Ken. *Knowing Jazz: Community, Pedagogy, and Canon in the Information Age.* Jackson, MS: University Press of Mississippi, 2012.

Quinn, Bernadette. "Arts Festivals and the City." *Urban Studies* 42, nos. 5–6 (2005): 927–43.

Rauscher, Frances H., and Sean C. Hinton. "Music Instruction and Its Diverse Extra-musical Benefits." *Music Perception* 29, no. 2 (2011): 215–26.

Reardon-Smith, Hannah, Louise Denson, and Vanessa Tomlinson. "Feministing Free Improvisation." *Tempo* 74, no. 292 (2020): 10–20.

Reason Myers, Dana. "The Myth of Absence: Representation, Reception, and the Music of Experimental Women Improvisors." PhD diss., University of California, San Diego, 2002.

Regis, Helen, and Shana Walton. "Producing the Folk at the New Orleans Jazz and Heritage Festival." *Journal of American Folklore* 121, no. 482 (Fall 2008): 400–440.

Robinson, Dylan. "To All Who Should Be Concerned." *Intersections* 39, no. 1 (2019): 137–44.

Rollins, Sonny. "Interview: Sonny Rollins (Part 3)." Interview by Marc Myers. *JazzWax.* February 21, 2008. https://www.jazzwax.com/2008/02/sonny-rolli ns-2.html

Rollins, Sonny. Interview by Tavis Smiley. *The Tavis Smiley Show.* PBS. September 26, 2011.

Roy, Arundhati. "The Pandemic Is a Portal." *Financial Times.* April 3, 2020. https://www.ft.com/content/10d8f5e8-74eb-11ea-95fe-fcd274e920ca

Said, Edward W. *Humanism and Democratic Criticism.* New York: Columbia University Press, 2004.

Said, Edward W. *Representations of the Individual.* New York: Vintage, 1996.

Salzman, Marian. "What's Next for Places?" *Huffington Post.* January 2, 2013. https://news.yahoo.com/whats-next-places-143303265.html

San Juan, E., Jr. *Racism and Cultural Studies: Critiques of Multiculturalist Ideology and the Politics of Difference.* Durham, NC: Duke University Press, 2002.

Sarath, Ed. "Founder's Message." International Society for Improvised Music. Accessed June 6, 2020. https://improvisedmusic.org/about-isim/

Sawyer, Keith. *Group Genius: The Creative Power of Collaboration.* New York: Basic Books, 2008.

Scherstuhl, Alan. "The Irreducible William Parker." *New York Times.* February 8, 2021. https://www.nytimes.com/2021/02/08/arts/music/william-parker-to ne-world.html

Smith, Leo. "American Music." *Black Perspective in Music* 2, no. 2 (1974): 111–16.

Solnit, Rebecca. *A Paradise Built in Hell: The Extraordinary Communities That Arise in Disaster.* New York: Viking, 2009.

Sommer, Doris. *The Work of Art in the World: Civic Agency and Public Humanities.* Durham, NC: Duke University Press, 2014.

Stewart, Jesse. "Freedom Music: Jazz and Human Rights." In *Rebel Musics: Human Rights, Resistant Sounds, and the Politics of Music Making,* edited by Daniel Fischlin and Ajay Heble, 88–107. Montreal: Black Rose, 2003.

Stewart, Jesse. "Hamid Drake: Drum Talk." *Cadence* 30, no. 3 (2004): 5–11.

Stewart, Jesse. "Improvisation Pedagogy in Theory and Practice." In *Improvisation and Music Education: Beyond the Classroom,* edited by Ajay Heble and Mark Laver, 32–45. New York: Routledge, 2016.

Stewart, Jesse. "Intervections." *Contemporary Music Review* 29, no. 3 (2010): 323–35.

Stewart, Jesse, Sherrie Tucker, Kip Haaheim, and Pete Williams. "AUMI-Futurism: The Elsewhere and 'Elsewhen' of *(Un)Rolling the Boulder* and *Turning the Page.*" *Music and Arts in Action* 6, no. 1 (2017): 4–24.

Sweet, Robert. *Music Universe, Music Mind: Revisiting the Creative Music Studio.* Ann Arbor, MI: Arborville, 1996.

Thompson, Amanda Karioth. "Leon Teacher's Unscripted Theater a Lesson in Coping with COVID Pandemic." *Tallahassee Democrat.* July 28, 2020. https:// www.tallahassee.com/story/life/family/2020/07/28/leon-teachers-unscript ed-theater-lesson-coping-covid/5519941002/

Thomson, Scott. "The Pedagogical Imperative of Musical Improvisation." *Critical Studies in Improvisation / Études critiques en improvisation* 3, no. 2 (2007). https://www.criticalimprov.com/index.php/csieci/article/view/353/643

Tomlinson, Barbara, and George Lipsitz. *Insubordinate Spaces: Improvisation and Accompaniment for Social Justice.* Philadelphia: Temple University Press, 2019.

Truth and Reconciliation Commission of Canada. "Truth and Reconciliation Commission of Canada: Calls to Action." 2015. http://trc.ca/assets/pdf/Calls_to_Action_English2.pdf

"Twelfth Annual Girls' Jazz & Blues Camp." California Jazz Conservatory. Accessed June 6, 2020. https://cjc.edu/jazzschool/intensives/summer-youth-programs/girls-jazz-blues-camp/

Uitti, Frances-Marie. "Preserving the Scelsi Improvisations." *Tempo,* no. 194 (1995): 12–14.

United Nations. *Plan of Action, World Program for Human Rights Education.* Paris: UNESCO, 2006. https://www.ohchr.org/Documents/Publications/PActionEducationen.pdf

Varvarigou, Maria, Andrea Creech, Susan Hallam, and Hilary McQueen. "Bringing Different Generations Together in Music-Making: An Intergenerational Music Project in East London." *International Journal of Community Music* 4, no. 3 (2011): 207–20.

Wallace, Rob. "Terrorism and the Politics of Improvisation." In *The Politics of Post-9/11 Music: Sound Trauma and the Music Industry,* edited by Joseph P. Fisher and Brian Flota, 79–92. Wey Court East: Ashgate, 2011.

Warwick, Jacqueline. "Music Education Has a Race Problem, and Universities Must Address It." *The Conversation.* August 9, 2020. https://theconversation.com/music-education-has-a-race-problem-and-universities-must-address-it-143719

Weiss, Jason. *Steve Lacy: Conversations.* Durham, NC: Duke University Press, 2006.

Whaley, John, John Sloboda, and Alf Gabrielsson. "Peak Experiences in Music." In *Oxford Handbook of Music Psychology,* edited by Susan Hallam, Ian Cross, and Michael Thaut, 452–61. Oxford: Oxford University Press, 2009.

Whyton, Tony. "Birth of the School: Discursive Methodologies in Jazz Education." *Music Education Research* 8, no. 1 (2006): 65–81.

Williams, James Gordon. *Crossing Bar Lines: The Politics and Practices of Black Musical Space.* Jackson: University Press of Mississippi, 2021.

Wilson, Carl. "A Rhapsody for Guelph's Motherlode of Jazz, 10th Anniversary Edition." *Globe and Mail.* September 4, 2003. https://www.theglobeandmail.com/arts/a-rhapsody-for-guelphs-motherlode-of-jazz/article772118/

Wyman, Max. *The Defiant Imagination: Why Culture Matters.* Vancouver: Douglas and McIntyre, 2004.

Wynn, Jonathan. *Music/City: American Festivals and Placemaking in Austin, Nashville, and Newport.* Chicago: University of Chicago Press, 2015.

Zournazi, Mary. *Hope: New Philosophies for Change.* New York: Routledge, 2003.

Select Discography of Improvised Music

The following discography complements the one compiled by George Lewis for his 1996 essay "Improvised Music after 1950." Although neither list is exhaustive, when taken together they provide an admittedly selective, yet thorough and wide-ranging, introduction to the recorded histories of creative improvised music to date and many of the key contributors therein.

Muhal Richard Abrams, George Lewis, and Roscoe Mitchell. *Streaming.* PI Recordings (PI22), 2006.

Susan Alcorn, Ingrid Laubrock, Leila Bordreuil. *Bird Meets Wire.* Relative Pitch Records (RPR 1098), 2021.

Susan Alcorn, Joe McPhee, Ken Vandermark. *Invitation to a Dream.* Astral Spirits (AS100LP), 2019.

Hossein Alizadeh and Madjid Khaladj. *25 Years of Extraordinary Collaboration, Vol. 1.* Ba Music Records, 2017.

jaimie branch. *Fly or Die.* International Anthem Recording Co. (IARC0011-CD), 2017.

Anthony Braxton and Fred Frith. *Duo (Victoriaville) 2005.* Les Disques Victo (VICTO CD 100), 2006.

Peter Brötzmann, Maâlem Moukhtar Gania, and Hamid Drake. *The Catch of a Ghost.* I Dischi di Angelica (IDA041), 2020.

Marilyn Crispell, Fred Anderson, and Hamid Drake. *Destiny.* Okka Disk (OD12003), 1996.

Marilyn Crispell, Peter Brötzmann, and Hamid Drake. *Hyperion.* Music & Arts (CD-852), 1995.

Jen Curtis and Tyshawn Sorey. *Invisible Ritual.* Tundra (Tun014), 2020.

Jean Derome, Malcolm Goldstein, and Rainer Wiens. *6 Improvisations.* Ambiances Magnétiques (AM 214), 2013.

Hamid Drake and Joe McPhee. *Emancipation Proclamation: A Real Statement of Freedom.* Okka Disk (OD12036), 2000.

Douglas Ewart. *Bamboo Meditations at Banff.* Aarawak Recording (AA003), 1994.

Jaron Freeman-Fox. *Manic Almanac: Slow Möbius.* Self-released, 2010.

Fred Frith, Anne Bourne, and John Oswald. *Dearness.* Spool (SPL 116), 2001.

Fushitsusha. *A Death Never to Be Complete.* J-Factory (TKCF-77014), 1997.

Ganelin / Tarasov / Chekasin. *Live in East Germany.* Leo Records (LR 102), 1980.

Virginia Genta. *Rough Enough.* Holidays Records (HOL 092), 2016.

Glasgow Improvisers Orchestra, featuring Marilyn Crispell and Evan Parker. *Parallel Moments Unbroken.* FMR Records (FMRCD520–1018), 2018.

Gordon Grdina, François Houle, Kenton Loewen, and Benoît Delbecq. *Ghost Lights.* Songlines Recordings (SGL 1621–2), 2017.

Keiji Haino and John Butcher. *Light Never Bright Enough.* Otoroku (ROKU018), 2017.

Mary Halvorson Octet. *Away with You.* Firehouse 12 (FH12-04-08-024), 2016.

Susie Ibarra. *Flower after Flower.* Tzadik Records (TZ 7057), 2000.

Susie Ibarra Trio. *Radiance.* Hopscotch Records (HOP 2), 1999.

ICP Orchestra. *Jubilee Varia.* hatOLOGY (hatOLOGY 528), 1999.

Irreversible Entanglements. *Irreversible Entanglements.* International Anthem (IARC 0014), 2017.

Vijay Iyer and Wadada Leo Smith. *A Cosmic Rhythm with Each Stroke.* ECM Records (ECM 2486), 2016.

Keith Jarrett. *La Fenice.* ECM Records (ECM 2601/02), 2018.

Yusef Lateef, Roscoe Mitchell, Adam Rudolph, and Douglas R. Ewart. *Voice Prints.* Meta Records (018), 2013.

Ingrid Laubrock and Aki Takase. *Kasumi.* Intakt (Intakt CD 337), 2019.

Philippe Lauzier and Éric Normand. *Not the Music / Do.* Tour de Bras (TDB90022cd), 2014.

Joëlle Léandre and Nicole Mitchell. *Sisters Where.* RogueArt (ROG-0055), 2014.

George Lewis, Wadada Leo Smith, and John Zorn. *Sonic Rivers.* Tzadik Records (TZ4001), 2014.

Rob Mazurek and Black Cube SP. *Return the Tides: Ascension Suite and Holy Ghost.* Cuneiform Records (Rune 399), 2014.

Joe McPhee and John Heward. *Voices: 10 Improvisations.* Mode Avant, 2008.

Moskus. *Salmesykkel.* Hubro (HUBROCD2518), 2012.

The Necks. *Hanging Gardens.* Fish of Milk (FOM 0006), 1999.

Pauline Oliveros. *The Roots of the Moment.* hat ART (hat ART CD 6009), 1988.

Pauline Oliveros / Miya Masaoka. *Accordion Koto.* Deep Listening (DL 36–2007), 2007.

Evan Parker. *Whitstable Solo.* psi (psi 10.01), 2008.

Evan Parker, Derek Bailey, and Han Bennink. *The Topography of the Lungs.* Incus Records (INCUS.1), 1970. (Rereleased on psi in 2006.)

William Parker. *Crumbling in the Shadows Is Fraulein Miller's Stale Cake* (box set). Centering Records (1005/1006/1007), 2011.

William Parker & The Little Huey Creative Music Orchestra. *Sunrise in the Tone World.* AUM Fidelity (AUM 002/3), 1997.

William Parker and Raining on the Moon. *Corn Meal Dance.* AUM Fidelity (AUM043), 2007.

Phantom Orchard (Ikue Mori and Zeena Parkins). *Orra.* Tzadik (TZ 7718), 2008.

Eddie Prévost and John Butcher. *Visionary Fantasies.* Matchless Recordings (MRCD100), 2018.

Matana Roberts. *Coin Coin Chapter Three: River Run Thee.* Constellation (CST110–2), 2015.

Irène Schweizer. *To Whom It May Concern: Piano Solo Tonhalle Zürich.* Intakt Records (Intakt CD 200), 2011.

Sam Shalabi, Norman Adams, and Tim Crofts. *Collateral.* Self-released, 2016.

Supersilent. *6.* Rune Grammofon (RCD 2029), 2003.

Tanya Tagaq. *Retribution.* Six Shooter Records (SIXLP102), 2016.

Thumbscrew (Michael Formanek / Tomas Fujiwara / Mary Halvorson). *Ours.* Cuneiform Records (RUNE 439), 2018.

Trifolia. *Le Refuge.* Self-released, 2013.

David S. Ware & Matthew Shipp Duo. *Live in Sant'Anna Arresi, 2004.* AUM Fidelity (AUM 100), 2016.

Patty Waters. *The Complete ESP-Disk Recordings.* ESP-Disk (ESP 4019), 2006.

Index